Our Husband Has Gone Mad Again

Our Husband Has Gone Mad Again

— a comedy —

by

Ola Rotimi

**UNIVERSITY PRESS PLC
IBADAN**

University Press PLC
IBADAN ABUJA AKURE BENIN ENUGU ILORIN JOS
KANO LAGOS OWERRI UYO ZARIA

© Oxford University Press 1977
© University Press PLC 1999

ISBN-13: 978-978-154-003-5
ISBN 978 154003 6
Reprinted 1979, 1999

Printed by Automatic Printing Press Ltd., Ibadan
Published by University Press PLC
Three Crowns Building, P.M.B. 5095, Jericho, Ibadan, Nigeria

For

Hazel Mae

– the one who tries . . .

THE CHARACTERS

RAHMAN TASLIM LEJOKA-BROWN — alias: 'Di Major'

GIDEON ABEDNEGO OKONKWO — a lawyer and friend of Lejoka-Brown

MAMA RASHIDA — wife to Lejoka-Brown

SIKIRA — wife to Lejoka-Brown

LIZA — American-educated wife to Lejoka-Brown

ALHAJI MUSTAFA — a neighbour and a venerable old man

POLYCARP — steward in the Lejoka-Brown household

MALLAM GASKIYA — member of the National Liberation Party

MUSA OSAGIE — member of the National Liberation Party

MADAM BAMBINA AJANAKU — mother of Sikira and head of the National Union of Nigerian Market Women

BBC CORRESPONDENT

2 NIGERIAN JOURNALISTS

1 PRESS PHOTOGRAPHER

CROWD: members of the Nigerian National Liberation Party
members of the National Union of Nigerian Market Women
blustering party supporters, fair-weather cheerleaders, brawny party thugs.

This play was first performed at Yale University, Connecticut, U.S.A., as a major production of the Yale School of Drama in 1966, under the direction of the late award-winning American director, Jack Landau.

SETTING

LAGOS, amidst the hustle and bustle of political campaigns for General Elections in Nigeria.

The main action takes place in Major Lejoka-Brown's antiquated, wattle and clay-walled home – a standing wonder of 19th Century indigenous architecture.

Other happenings occur at the Ikeja International Airport, Lagos, and at the Conference Room of Major Lejoka-Brown's National Liberation Party – either of which can be scenically represented by simple panels bearing such inscriptions as:

LAGOS INTERNATIONAL AIRPORT

– No smoking –

and

NATIONAL LIBERATION PARTY

Conference Room

– Silence –

Outstanding Objects in Lejoka-Brown's Living-room

Displayed proudly on the walls are: a large map of Nigeria; an old matchet in its sheath, and a number of political posters proclaiming the varied slogans of the Nigerian National Liberation Party.

Furniture comprises some chairs; a settee; pouffes; a couple of drinks-tables; a record player, and a white sheepskin sprawling unconcernedly on the floor.

ATMOSPHERE

Campaign procession of Lejoka-Brown's National Liberation Party. Loud drumming and singing. Excited spectators converge from everywhere to applaud the banner-flaunting partisans.

Towering in the crowd is Major Lejoka-Brown himself, lavishly adorned in gaudy traditional attire complete with an *abeti aja* cap of the same *aso oke* fabric.

The index and forefinger of his right hand held up in a "Victory" sign, a mascot in the other hand, Major Lejoka-Brown responds with buoyant dignity to the cheering underlings! They cheer, he upholds his "V" and the good-luck pet (which happens to to be a baby python).

Drumming. Singing. Cheering.

Party Song

Chorus: Freedom, freedom,
Everywhere there must be freedom.

Solo: Freedom for you
Freedom for me

Chorus: Everywhere there must be freedom.

Solo: Freedom for Nigeria
Freedom for Africa

Chorus: Yes, everywhere there must be freedom.

All: Freedom, freedom,
Everywhere there must be freedom.

This song is counterpointed by the aggressively vociferous, coarse chanting of the party thugs.

Agẹmọ o se jẹ	The chameleon is no food.
Agẹmọ o se jẹ	Indeed
Ẹni ba f'ori sọ'lẹ a f'oju sọ'kun	The chameleon is no delicacy.
	The impact of the human head on hard ground commands tears from the eyes!
Lejoka-Brown l'anteriba fun	The reality of Lejoka-Brown's presence itself commands instant awe!
Igi t'o l'owun yio f'oju di ajanaku	A tree that seeks a taste of brute humiliation
A fori s'ọlẹ, erin a gori rẹ k'ọja	may dare the reality of an elephant
A k'ọri s'igbo	in a headlong thrust!
Agẹmọ o se jẹ.	Indeed the chameleon is no food!

Some of the parti-coloured banners exhort the populace to:

VOTE FOR FREEDOM NOW
OR FOREVER BE SLAVES!

VOTE FOR THE NATIONAL
LIBERATION PARTY
VOTE THE FREEDOM WAY.

REMEMBER THE VOTING DAY
AND KEEP IT NLP.

Others flaunt promises:

GOD MADE US
WE MAKE GOOD LIFE.

NATIONAL LIBERATION PARTY
SHALL MAKE YOU FREE.

OUR GOVERNMENT SHALL PRESERVE
YOUR FATHERS' HOUSES.

YOU BEAR THE CHILDREN
WE PAY THEIR SCHOOLING.

YOU TOO CAN CHOP LIFE
JUST VOTE NLP.

LIKE PROPHET MUHAMMAD,
OUR GOVERNMENT
WILL COME TO YOU.

WE WILL GIVE YOU
FREEDOM OF BIRTH
AND LIFE AS RICH AS
ROLLS-ROYCE.

Procession may progress through the audience and exit through side-doors. To achieve an initial warm, audience-actor rapport, it is suggested that handbills proclaiming the hopes and aspirations detailed above be handed out to the audience by the actors/actresses on parade.

ACT 1

ACT 1

SCENE I

LEJOKA-BROWN'S *living-room*. SIKIRA *clad in buba and wrapper, with a veil fluffing loosely about her neck and shoulders, is sitting, legs wide apart, on the settee, listlessly eating an orange, and making mouths.*

SIKIRA [*as if addressing the orange*]. Has my lord finished eating?

[*But the question seems unnecessary, as we now hear footsteps in martial rhythm approaching.* SIKIRA *quickly drapes the veil over her face and prinks herself up. Meanwhile, an imperious baritone is intoning in time with the marching.*]

LEJOKA-BROWN [*offstage*]. Ah lef, ah lef, ah lef rai ah lef compana-a-, go!

[*A baritone and tenor duet croons lustily.*]

LEJOKA-BROWN AND OKONKWO [*approaching*].
Ai remembah when ai was a soljar,
Ai remembah when ai was a soljar,
Ai remembah when ai was a soljar,
Ai remembah when ai was a soljar,

[LEJOKA-BROWN AND OKONKWO *march into the living-room.*]

Hippy ya ya, hippy hippy ya-ya,
Hippy ya ya, hippy hippy ya-ya,
Hippy ya ya, hippy hippy ya-ya,
Hippy ya ya, hippy hippy ya-ya,

[SIKIRA *kneels in greeting. The* MAJOR *responds with a quick side glance, then changes the marching tune.*]
Leave your wife and join di army
One more rivah to cross:
One more rivah,
One more rivah,
One more rivah,
To cross.

[*The sharp contrast in dress and physique of these two men strikes us immediately.* MAJOR LEJOKA-BROWN, *husky, broad-shouldered, barrel-chested and hirsute, has only a loin-cloth on, buttressing, as it were, the complacent sag of his jumbo-sized potbelly. Lawyer* OKONKWO, *on the other hand, is spruced up in a Western suit that lends some dignity to his frail, five-foot-five frame.* OKONKWO *is sipping a drink from a bottle in his left hand;* LEJOKA-BROWN *carouses his palmwine direct from a gourd. They sing on, in nostalgic insouciance, march-drilling round the living-room.*]

Home again, home again
When shall ai see my home?
When shall ai see my native land?
Ai'll nevah forget my home.

[*They halt, come to attention and salute.*]

LEJOKA-BROWN. As you were!

[*They relax, strike bottle against gourd, drink; then burst into laughter, amused by their own antics.*]

OKONKWO. Major Rahman Lejoka-Brown! [*Slaps him robustly on the back.*] Yarn me boh! Ehen, so you're now in full time politics!

LEJOKA-BROWN. Are you there . . . ? politics is the thing now in Nigeria, mate. You want to be famous? Politics. You want to chop life? – No, no – you want to chop a big slice of the National cake? – Na Politics. [*Clears his throat.*] So I said to my party boys – when was it? Last week, or so. I said to them . . . I said: [*Striking an oratorical pose.*] Cakes are too soft, Gentlemen. Just you wait! Once we get elected to the top, *wallahi**, we shall stuff ourselves with huge mouthfuls of the National chin-chin [*Munches an imaginary mouthful.*] something you'll eat and eat, brothers, and you know you've eaten something.

[*They both laugh, slouching in the settee.*]

* Refer to the Glossary for all words or expressions marked with an *.

LEJOKA-BROWN. Abi? Yoruba man say: "man-u way go chop-u frog, make he kuku chop-u di frog-u way get-i egg-i for belle!" Abi, no be so?

OKONKWO. Major Rahman Lejoka-Brown Esquire!

[LEJOKA-BROWN *pops up suddenly.*]

LEJOKA-BROWN. Hey, remember this one? Look ... hep ... hep ... [*he is attempting an exercise: an arm stretched out and forward, the opposite leg kicking high to touch hand with foot.* SIKIRA *sniggers as her husband strains to impress.*]

OKONKWO. Enough, Major, look – your wife is laughing at you!

LEJOKA-BROWN [*still at it*]. Hep ... a woman ... hep ... an ordinary – hep ... woman! What does she know – hep ... hep ... about army ... hep ... exercise? – hep ... As for you – hep ... six years in England – hep ... has made you – hep ... soft like a ... hep – woman!

[*puffing, seizes* OKONKWO *by the arm, confronts* SIKIRA.]

Are you ... there ...? Wife! Do you see this man, or don't you? Now, I know you think he is one of those tiny little Sanitary Inspectors who come here every Wednesday morning to peep in your water-pots in search of mosquito eggs!

SIKIRA. Ooh no, my lord, I wasn't thinking so –

LEJOKA-BROWN. Y-e-s, go ahead: think – think whatever you want to think. [*Hoists* OKONKWO'S *arm up.*] This man here is that same brave soldier, Gideon Abednego Okonkwo, who fought shoulder to shoulder with me in the Congo against those long-nosed Belgians during ...

SIKIRA [*impressed*]. Ohoo!

[MAMA RASHIDA *enters from outside. Balanced on her head is a large basket-cage housing a number of live chickens. She is just returning from the market.*]

LEJOKA-BROWN [*with a broad sweep of the arm that takes in both* SIKIRA *and* MAMA RASHIDA]. Wives ...

OKONKWO [*confused*]. Hunh?

LEJOKA-BROWN [*indicating both women again*]. I said: Wives ... [*Clears his throat.*] Wives ... he is a lawyer now.

SIKIRA AND MAMA RASHIDA. E-he-en!

LEJOKA-BROWN. H-e-en, just returned from ... [*hiccups*] from England. Are you there ...? So you take good care of him whenever he comes here.

SIKIRA AND MAMA RASHIDA. We will, my lord.
  [*They kneel in greeting and exit into the yard.* LEJOKA-BROWN *takes another swig of the palmwine, pats his stomach.*]
LEJOKA-BROWN. You're right, mate, fatness has begun to "monkey" with my body!
  [*Goes into another exercise, arms akimbo, bows forward, up, briskly to the right, up, left, up again, then forward etc.*]
OKONKWO. Di Major! Hey, when did you leave the army, by the way?
LEJOKA-BROWN [*going ahead with the exercise*]. Not long after you left. [*Calls*] Sikira!
SIKIRA [*offstage*]. Sah!
LEJOKA-BROWN [*continuing with the dialogue*]. Three months after I came back from the Congo. My father's cocoa farm was falling to pieces, so I resigned from the army to take it up, full-time.
OKONKWO. So how did you do?
LEJOKA-BROWN. You mean ... Where's the Sikira who answered "shaann" just now, na? –
SIKIRA [*entering*]. Here I am, my –
LEJOKA-BROWN. Towel, towel – get me a towel.
  [*She leaves to get it.*]
LEJOKA-BROWN [*continuing*]. Money-wise, I did very well. Cocoa business na money, o!
OKONKWO. Really?
  [SIKIRA *enters with a towel.* LEJOKA-BROWN *takes it, swabbing it liberally on his face, chest, armpits etc.*]
LEJOKA-BROWN. Wallahi Kalahi! If they put you on auction right now – you, your degrees, your coat – everything ... I can buy you ten times, and still have plenty money left to buy you all over again! But I'm pumping a lot of money into this election. Come here ...
  [*Spreads a map on a table.*]
In two weeks, my party begins a campaign throughout the country. Are you there ...?
  [*Calls again*]
Sikira!
SIKIRA [*offstage*]. Coming, my lord.
LEJOKA-BROWN. Don't come empty, o! Woman, I want two beers!
SIKIRA [*still shouting from offstage*]. I've heard you, my lord.

LEJOKA-BROWN. I'm directing the campaigns ...
   [*Barks out an after-thought at* SIKIRA.]
Are you there? Stout beer, woman – stout beer. Two.
   [*To* OKONKWO.]
Stout beer is good for the heart! Dem say. Now, I'm directing my Party campaigns myself. How?
POLYCARP [*off stage*]. Major!
LEJOKA-BROWN. I am using army tactics – surprise and attack!
OKONKWO. Surprise and wh-a-at?
LEJOKA-BROWN. Surprise and attack.
   [SIKIRA *enters with drinks, stands them on table and exits.*]
POLYCARP [*still offstage*]. Major!
   [*Enter* POLYCARP, *clad in khaki shirt over a pair of shorts of the same fabric. In his hand is a cablegram. A pair of worn-out army boots encases his feet, like over sized hooves.*]
POLYCARP. Major!
LEJOKA-BROWN [*about to demonstrate his plan to* OKONKWO]. Are you there ...? This is how it works. I send ...
POLYCARP [*saluting*]. Beg to report, sah ...
LEJOKA-BROWN [*still engrossed in his plan*]. Some Party men to ...
POLYCARP. Major!
LEJOKA-BROWN [*irritated by this interruption, whirls round and, wielding a bottle, capers threateningly toward* POLYCARP].
The god of iron stuff this bottle down your noisy throat!
POLYCARP [*holding out cablegram*]. Cablegram, Sir!
   [LEJOKA-BROWN *snatches cablegram from him and starts prying the envelope open.*]
OKONKWO. It sounds like war.
LEJOKA-BROWN. It is war! Politics is war. Oooh – I am taking no chances this time, brother mine. Mhm. Last time, I took things slow and easy and what happened? Chuu! I lost a by-election to a ... a small crab ... a baby monkey.
   [*Winkles paper out of envelope, and starts unfolding it.*]
Mhm. This time it is war!
   [*Reads cable; the contents are disconcerting.*]
Unsurni ya Allah!*
OKONKWO. Bad news?
LEJOKA-BROWN. Gamalin-20!
OKONKWO. Your politics?
LEJOKA-BROWN. My wife.

OKONKWO. Your wh-a-at?

LEJOKA-BROWN. She's arriving at five o'clock!

OKONKWO. Arriving?

LEJOKA-BROWN. From America!

OKONKWO. America? Another wife?

LEJOKA-BROWN [*angrily*]. What's her rush, anyway? Cablegram after cablegram after cablegram, I sent to her: "Wait, Liza, don't come now. Wait till elections are over before you ..."

OKONKWO. Major I don't get ...

LEJOKA-BROWN. Now she'll come mess things up *jagajaga** for me, my party ...

OKONKWO. Major ...

LEJOKA-BROWN. Everybody will be saying ...

OKONKWO. You ... have a third wife?

LEJOKA-BROWN. Hunh? No no, no – this woman who is arriving from America is not my *third* wife.

OKONKWO. Oh, I thought you said ...

LEJOKA-BROWN. She is my *second* wife ...

OKONKWO. Hunh?

LEJOKA-BROWN. Although she thinks she's the *first*, but that's beside the point.

OKONKWO. You mean she doesn't know you already have two other wives?

[LEJOKA-BROWN *shakes his head mournfully*.]

Well ... [*uncertainly*] maybe ... if she is like you – a Muslim – she would understand.

LEJOKA-BROWN [*vacantly*]. She's not a Muslim.

OKONKWO. No?

LEJOKA-BROWN. Catholic.

OKONKWO. A catholic!

LEJOKA-BROWN. The very worst!

OKONKWO. But major, how did you ...

LEJOKA-BROWN. I met her in Stanleyville during the Congo thing. I think by that time you had gone with another battalion to Luluaburg.

OKONKWO. I see.

LEJOKA-BROWN. One day, as our infantry was mopping up pockets of guerilla resistance – *cra-ka-ka-ka-ka-ka-ka-ka* – a Belgian mercenary coward fired SMG into my thigh. I was rushed to the hospital and Liza ...

[MAMA RASHIDA *enters with a tray of groundnuts.*]
Liza was a medical student – A Kenyan girl, helping the Red Cross. [*To a waiting* RASHIDA] Yes?
MAMA RASHIDA. What will my lord eat this evening?
LEJOKA-BROWN [*irritably*]. Nothing, nothing!
[MAMA RASHIDA *places tray on table, exits.*]
She took very good care of me at the hospital. Two months after, we went to the Marriage Registry and...fixed things up.
OKONKWO. A Court Marriage! Major – with another wife hidden away here in Lagos?
LEJOKA-BROWN. I didn't know I had another wife.
OKONKWO [*chuckles incredulously*]. Oh, come now!
LEJOKA-BROWN. *Wallahi*! [*raises a hand piously*] Mama Rashida? Mama Rashida was the oldest of my late brother's wives. See? My older brother – Peace of Allah on his soul – he died in a train accident. Two days before my marriage to Liza, I got a letter from my father. Oh, he had taken pity on Mama Rashida, he said, and had gone ahead and married her off to me! Can you imagine that! Married the old woman off to me, while I, in the name of the United Nations, was in the Congo, busy collecting Belgian bullets in my belly!
OKONKWO [*tickled*]. Di major!
LEJOKA-BROWN. I mean, not that I don't like Mama Rashida as a person. I like her and respect her – in many ways she is just like Liza herself – you know – well-mannered, quiet, full of concern: a well-bred, African pigeon. But... are you there...? I mean... let's face it... you know... look at it... I mean... you see...
OKONKWO. All the same, you should have explained to Liza long before this... this...
LEJOKA-BROWN. Welcome! An intelligent girl like Liza, with only two days before our marriage, and she preparing to go to America on a Kenyan Government scholarship to get a special degree in medicine. I walk up to her: "Darling...
[SIKIRA *enters at this point unseen by Lejoka-Brown.*]
...darling, I want you to be my wife, but you will be wife number One-B. Why? Because wife number One-A, just married to me by my father, is at..." [*sees* SIKIRA.] What's your trouble?
SIKIRA. Polycarp said you got a cablegram. I hope it is nothing bad.

LEJOKA-BROWN. Thanks for your concern!

[SIKIRA *lingers on, which irks* LEJOKA-BROWN.] I said thanks for your concern. A-ah! Polycarp brought a cablegram, yes. Is your name Rahman Lejoka-Brown?

SIKIRA [*teasingly polite*]. Sorry sah.

[*Curtseys and exits.*]

LEJOKA-BROWN [*indicating* SIKIRA]. I married that Problem only four months ago.

OKONKWO [*accusingly*]. Without telling Liza either!

LEJOKA-BROWN. Her marriage is for emergency, in order that...

[*defensively.*]

What type of question are you asking anyhow? "Why didn't I tell Liza; why didn't I tell" – What's the matter? Does a man have to broadcast to one wife every time he marries a new one?

[*lowering his voice*]

That woman's case is only for necessity, anyway – temporary measure. We need women's votes, man, if we must win the next elections.

OKONKWO. And what would one extra woman do to win you those votes?

LEJOKA-BROWN. She is the daughter of the President of the Nigerian Union of Market Women.

OKONKWO. Oooh.

LEJOKA-BROWN [*triumphantly*]. See what I mean? Everything would have worked out according to plan once the elections were over. See? I give Sikira lump sum capital to go and trade and look for another man or something like that; Mama Rashida remains right in this house of my fathers; and I move into Minister's quarters on Victoria Island. Liza joins me there: everybody is happy. But now look at it.

[*Flings the cablegram at* OKONKWO.]

OKONKWO. Better do something quick man.

LEJOKA-BROWN. What? What can I do? Read it! She hardly gives a man time to think!

[*Picks up cablegram again.*]

Arriving today Friday 21st. 5.00 p.m. All right, so she has graduated this month. But I wrote to her: "elections are getting me very busy, 'Lizabeth. Take a long holiday: go to Rome, visit Paris, come to Nigeria after the elections."

I even sent her eight hundred pounds to make sure she went to Rome, Paris or places like that. Now she is using that damned money to fly straight into my secrets!

OKONKWO. Hey... I'll tell you what...

LEJOKA-BROWN. What?

OKONKWO. Send the two women away for the time being.

LEJOKA-BROWN. To where? And what if Sikira's mother finds out that I have kicked her only daughter out of my house, so I can drag in my Ameriko? Chuu! Finish! That'll be the end of my politics!

OKONKWO. Okay, so you move out of this house, rent yourself a room somewhere, and rent another separate flat for Liza. That way you can still have all the women and not make one suspect that you are favouring the other.

LEJOKA-BROWN. What are you talking about? [*aghast.*] You mean, I should live alone? What are you talking about?

OKONKWO. Till the elections are over, then you can sort things out!

LEJOKA-BROWN. In other words, I should live all by myself for six whole months?

[*Shrugs his shoulders.*]

L a rahbaniyya fil Islam!*

OKONKWO. Who says you can't go visiting the women?

LEJOKA-BROWN. [*becoming sarcastic*]. In their separate hotels?

OKONKWO. Who is talking about hotels?

LEJOKA-BROWN. Well, isn't that what it comes to? I leave these two women here in Idumagbo; next, I hire room and parlour in Surulere for Liza; then I, too, bury my head in a separate room at Abule 'jesha. Abi? I wake up every morning and parade from one house to another visiting these women. That's right! Suddenly, I'm no more a husband; I've become a caretaker! Thank you!

OKONKWO. Look, don't bite me, Major – after all it was only a suggestion. J-e-e-sus wept!

LEJOKA-BROWN [*hotly*]. So stop making funny suggestions, brother, I'm in trouble: I mean, look at it – I should leave my women open, unprotected, each one camped in a separate tent, while *I* hide myself away for six whole donkey months – what do you think I am? IMPOTENT?

[*Moves away.*]

OKONKWO. All right, Major ... I'm sorry ...
[*empties his glass and goes to* LEJOKA-BROWN.]
Shake hands, mate – I've got to go!

LEJOKA-BROWN [*alarmed*]. You're coming with me to the airport, you know!

OKONKWO. Why?

LEJOKA-BROWN. OK ... let's put it this way. Are you there ...? Your suggestion is crazy, and yet not crazy ...
[*puts a hand on* OKONKWO's *shoulder and leads him coaxingly back to his seat.*]
Now suppose, instead of renting a separate flat for Liza and me alone ... suppose ... are you there? Suppose I get a flat immediately and move into it with Liza – just the two of us, while these other women remain in the dignity and protection of this house of my fathers. How is that?
[*Calls.*]
Mama Rashida!

OKONKWO [*non-committally*]. OK.

LEJOKA-BROWN. I might as well –
[MAMA RASHIDA *enters.*]

MAMA RASHIDA. Did my lord call ...?

LEJOKA-BROWN. Yes ... mmm ... your ... I've had a cablegram ... your, mmm ... sister-in-marriage is arriving this evening.

MAMA RASHIDA. Our sister-in-marriage?

LEJOKA-BROWN. The one in America.

MAMA RASHIDA. Ohoo! Sister Liza! So, at last we shall be seeing her – heyyy. May Allah bring her safely to us, o!
[SIKIRA *is attracted by the jubilant exclamations.*]

SIKIRA [*bursting in*]. Who is Allah bringing, o?

LEJOKA-BROWN [*to* MAMA RASHIDA]. Get me my blue damask.
[MAMA RASHIDA *hurries off.*]

SIKIRA [*going after* MAMA RASHIDA]. Who is Allah bringing?

LEJOKA-BROWN [*to* OKONKWO]. See what I mean? It's not "Who is coming, o?" No. To her, it has to be "Who is Allah bringing?"

OKONKWO. But why did you tell them?

LEJOKA-BROWN. Much better that way.

OKONKWO [*baffled*]. But the whole purpose of wanting to live apart with Liza is to keep these women from knowing!

LEJOKA-BROWN. No, no – it's better for them to know. It is

the meeting between them that must be blocked. See? Now they can understand when I suddenly begin to disappear from here. And if they start complaining – "Oh, but I told you both that Liza had arrived, didn't I? Or don't you want me to keep her company?" [*mimicking*] "We do, my lord, but..." "Well it's not my fault, if Liza prefers to live outside, is it?" That takes care of that!

[MAMA RASHIDA *enters and hands him the blue dress – a set of* "buba", "shokoto", "agbada" *and cap – then exits.*]

OKONKWO. Man, you'd better hurry up, if you have to get a flat rented, pack your things into it, and be at the airport before five o'clock!

LEJOKA-BROWN [*dressing*]. That's no problem. We'll stop at Maryland Estate on our way to the airport, and get a furnished flat. As for packing in, I'll start doing that tomorrow.

OKONKWO [*tickled*]. Won't Liza wonder why – all of a sudden you start moving in to join her, instead of her moving in to join you?

LEJOKA-BROWN. I'll say I've just got the place – specially for us. I'd been living in my grandfather's old house, which I didn't think she'd like. That's all.

OKONKWO. Suppose she decides to visit the grandfather's old house?

LEJOKA-BROWN. I'll bring her to visit this place.

OKONKWO. But then she'll see the women.

LEJOKA-BROWN. I'll brief her before we enter here: Mama Rashida is my sister; Sikira, my niece.

OKONKWO [*impressed by his resourcefulness*]. Di Major!

LEJOKA-BROWN. Only thing is, such visits will have to be brief. The briefer the better.

[*Enter* SIKIRA *again.*]

SIKIRA. Is my lord now going to pick up our new "Iyawo"* from the airport?

LEJOKA-BROWN [*a grunt*]. It is so.

SIKIRA [*childishly taunting*]. Hey! Will she be bringing us chewing-gum? Real, American chewing gum?

LEJOKA-BROWN. The briefer the better, I tell you. Oya – let's go.

[*They move off.*]

Mama Rashida, we're **going, o!**

MAMA RASHIDA [*running in, broom in hand*]. Go well, my lord.
SIKIRA [*cooing after* LEJOKA-BROWN]. My lord, tell sisi Liza to bring us balloons, too, o!

  SIKIRA *titters and flops on the settee, laughing naughtily.* MAMA RASHIDA *stands scowling down at her for a while then* ...

SCENE II

She gets on with the general clean-up of the living-room, while giving instructions to the house-boy, POLYCARP, *who has entered, carrying a pail and a broom.*
MAMA RASHIDA. When you finish, clean up the middle room.
POLYCARP. Yes ma.
MAMA RASHIDA. And lock Freedom up under the bed.
POLYCARP. Yes ma.
  [*A dull heavy crash occurs offstage.*]
MAMA RASHIDA. Arhamni Ya – Allah!*
SIKIRA [*excitedly*]. There goes another house!
  [POLYCARP *makes for the window to peep out, but is intercepted by* MAMA RASHIDA.]
MAMA RASHIDA. Go about your job, quick!
  [*She shoves him out through rear door.*]
SIKIRA [*peeping out*]. Mama Rashida, come look, come look!
  [MAMA RASHIDA, *disregarding* SIKIRA, *whisks her broom busily over the walls of the living-room.*]
SIKIRA. It's Alhaji Mustafa's house they're breaking down this time!
  [*Offstage – continuous heckling and catcalls punctuated by the ghoulish pounding of a demolition crane.*]
SIKIRA. Policemen with guns ... all over the place ... Oh, come see, quick ... they're fighting the people.
MAMA RASHIDA [*sternly*]. Sikira!
SIKIRA. What is it?
MAMA RASHIDA. The chairs, Woman, they need dusting ... the window-blinds, the chair covers must be ...
SIKIRA [*nonchalantly*]. Aaahh.
  [*She turns away to resume her gaze through the window.*]

MAMA RASHIDA. Now, you listen to me, Woman!
[*She seizes* SIKIRA *by the shoulder, yanks her away from the window, and shuts it, cutting off the noise from outside.* MAMA RASHIDA *and* SIKIRA *now stand face to face – the one indignant, hurt; the other defiant, unconcerned.*]

MAMA RASHIDA. It is not for *my* wedding, nor for the memorial ceremonies for the Departed Spirits of my forebears, that I am killing myself to get this house clean. Ooooh no, Woman! Our husband's wife is arriving *this* afternoon from America, and you know...

SIKIRA. Good news!

MAMA RASHIDA. It is *your* duty, just as it is my duty, to make sure that when the woman steps into this house, she has no doubt that it is real human beings who live in it, and not bush pigs!

SIKIRA. I don't care what she thinks!

MAMA RASHIDA. Unless you have no shame, you ought to care!

SIKIRA. Shame! My spit!
[*spits.*]
In this house? Ha! A slave, that's what I am. Did he marry me because he loves me, or because of his crazy politics? What do I care whether he wins politics or not? Shame indeed.
[*almost in tears.*]
You already have two children by his brother so your heart is peaceful.

MAMA RASHIDA. It is nobody's fault that *your* baby didn't come out to see the world. Things like that happen. All we can do is pray to Allah to send the right seed for your womb to the master.

SIKIRA. Will our husband care for me now that that Miss World is coming here?

MAMA RASHIDA [*lost*]. Miss World?

SIKIRA. That black-white woman who spent her whole life roaming the streets of America!

MAMA RASHIDA [*shocked*]. Liza?

SIKIRA. Must I spell out her name?

MAMA RASHIDA. May Allah have mercy on you!
[*An old man carrying a rifle shuffles tiredly toward Lejoka-Brown's house.*]

SIKIRA. Ha! I know her kind. They think because they've been

to England or to American-Toronto, they think they can come kick everybody round and round like a ... football.
[*Old man knocks on door.* MAMA RASHIDA *and* SIKIRA *freeze, apprehensive, listening. Another knock.*]

MAMA RASHIDA. Who is it?

MUSTAFA. It is me, Alhaji Mustafa.
[*Mama Rashida and Sikira primp themselves, fidget with their veils, in readiness for* ALHAJI MUSTAFA'S *entrance.*]

MAMA RASHIDA. You may come in now, my lord. The door is not locked.
[MUSTAFA, *a tall slender man who could pass for a grandfather, is wearing a bedraggled jumper that barely covers the top of a skimpy pair of Yoruba pantaloons. He is unshod: a rather mangy contrast to the saintly white, if threadbare, turban swathing his head and chin. His hands clasped round the barrel of a rifle,* MUSTAFA'S *back is turned to the barely open door, his head bowed glumly.*]

MUSTAFA. Are the bodies of my master's wives well covered up against temptation?

MAMA RASHIDA. We pray you, my lord ...
[MAMA RASHIDA *hurries over to* SIKIRA, *and fusses over her veil making sure her face is well shrouded – the ears included. This done, she steps back a couple of paces, sizes* SIKIRA *up critically, decides something more must be done. She goes to her again, stoops, tugs at the bottom of* SIKIRA'S *waist-cloth pulling this down to hide* SIKIRA'S *ankles.* MAMA RASHIDA *herself is conservatively cocooned in her clothing: only the hands are inescapably visible.*]

MAMA RASHIDA. You may come in now, my lord.
[*Still standing full-back to the door,* MUSTAFA *extends an arm, and feels for the doorknob behind him.*]

MUSTAFA. I'm coming in.
[*But he does not move.*]

MAMA RASHIDA. May your coming be blessed, my lord.
[MAMA RASHIDA *and* SIKIRA *kneel down on the sheepskin on the floor of the living-room.*]

MUSTAFA [*opening the door a little wider: pause*]. I'm almost in.
[*Door eases open daringly;* MUSTAFA *begins to inch his way in, backwards, his head still lowered, drooping: the caution of someone scrutinizing the floor in search of a precious tiny bit of lost jewel.*]

MUSTAFA [*only his rump within*]. I'm almost in now.

MAMA RASHIDA. Good day, my lord.
  [MUSTAFA *shuffles further into the living-room, still backwards. About eight paces in, he halts.*]
MUSTAFA. I am turning around.
SIKIRA [*with disgust*]. Good day, my lord!
MUSTAFA [*slowly turning around, his head still bowed*]. I will look at you now.
  [MUSTAFA *now faces the women.*]
  May Allah bring peace unto your hearts, Sisters.
MAMA RASHIDA AND SIKIRA. And unto your heart too my ...
MUSTAFA. The master ... is he not in?
MAMA RASHIDA. No, my lord.
MUSTAFA [*disappointed*]. That is bad!
MAMA RASHIDA. He went to the airport.
SIKIRA [*caustically*]. To bring our American 'yawo!
MAMA RASHIDA. Sshh!
  [*The women are now fascinated by Mustafa and the rifle he is wielding.*]
  I hope there is no trouble, my lord.
MUSTAFA. When a bald-headed man goes into the shop of a barber, his reason is not a haircut; it is another problem. Hmm ... there is trouble Sister. There is trouble. They have just broken down the house of my grandfather. Hmm. What the eyes see in this Lagos, the mouth can't describe. As if ... as if it was nothing ... the Government demons broke it down with their Whiteman's machine. It is a disgrace, Sisters. A horrible sight! I thought I could stop the devils. Somehow. So I borrowed the master's gun. But ... no use. Policemen, Policemen – all over the place. Three and twenty of them! All with guns. So I said to myself:
  "Alhaji Mustafa, you are crazy. You are only one man with only one gun; and out there, are three and twenty devils in uniform armed with three and twenty guns. Alhaji Mustafa get out of this place, o! Go away in peace. Hmm. Let the Spirits of your Dead Fathers fight for you." Toh!
  [*Hands rifle to* MAMA RASHIDA.]
  Tell the master not to try fighting the devils either, when they come to break down this house of his ancestors. No use.
  [*Turns to go.*]
  Tell the master that the Government devils gave me three

thousand pounds for my house. So let him not take a half-penny less for a place like this one.

[*Moving on.*]

I henceforth go to live in my father's farmland in Agege, o.

MAMA RASHIDA. Go well, my lord.

MUSTAFA [*stopping at the door*]. Oh ... how rude of me. [*Turns around.*] What time is the young lady arriving?

SIKIRA. Young lady – ha! The witch is old enough to be my grandmother!

MUSTAFA. I beg your pardon!

MAMA RASHIDA [*embarrassed*]. Fi-fi-five, my lord. She is arriving at five o'clock.

MUSTAFA. May Allah help you all to live together in peace and ...

SIKIRA [*grabbing a pouffe*]. Halleluyah! Ase!* [*Dropping it hard.*]

[MUSTAFA *and* MAMA RASHIDA *exchange glances;* MAMA RASHIDA *terribly horrified*, MUSTAFA *wondering what could be the cause of* SIKIRA'S *impudence. At last,* MUSTAFA *shakes his head resignedly, sighs, and steps out of the house, shutting the door courteously after him, as he mutters* ...]

MUSTAFA. Hmm. Children of these days – only Allah can save us. [*Exits.*]

MAMA RASHIDA [*incensed, to* SIKIRA]. Awful! Awful! Woman, awful!

POLYCARP [*offstage*]. Mama Rashida!

MAMA RASHIDA. Shame on you! Such rudeness – right in the presence of an Elder!

[*Removes her veil, and spits in contempt.*]

May Allah have mercy on you!

[POLYCARP, *pail in hand, bursts into the living-room.*]

POLYCARP. Mama Rashida – look for window. Quick ...

[*He crosses to a window.*]

MAMA RASHIDA. What is it?

POLYCARP. I think di iyawo done come, O!

MAMA RASHIDA. What?

POLYCARP. One taxi done come for front house.

SIKIRA [*peeping through window*]. Well, well, well ... look w! is here!

MAMA RASHIDA. You mean – Allah have mercy ...

[*Fluttering around, setting things in order.*]

and everything is still in a mess.

POLYCARP. Make I go tote her load, abi make I no go?
MAMA RASHIDA. Go, go, go – no, wait! Is her room ready?
POLYCARP. Ai done ready am, ma.
MAMA RASHIDA. Good, now run.
POLYCARP. But . . .
MAMA RASHIDA. What again?
POLYCARP. Freedom dey still sleep under master bed o.
MAMA RASHIDA [*angrily*]. I said lock him up in . . .
POLYCARP. I try, Mama Rashida, but every time I wan' catch 'am e dey make . . .
[*Wriggling in imitation of snake movement.*]
. . . yolopi – yolopi . . . yolopi – yolopi . . . yolo . . .
MAMA RASHIDA. All right, never mind, his master will take care of him later. You run quick and help bring in sister Liza's things!
[POLYCARP *scuttles off.*]
SIKIRA [*still peeping out*]. The master is not with her, o!
MAMA RASHIDA [*baffled*]. Not with her?
SIKIRA. I jo! What a dress she has on!
MAMA RASHIDA. Now, you listen to me, Woman . . .
[*Hurries up to* SIKIRA *wagging a warning finger.*]
Tell that hot, hot temper you have to go to the . . .
SIKIRA. I can even see her . . .
[SIKIRA *clears her throat obscenely followed by a hacking laugh as she pirouettes drunkenly to flop on the settee.*]
MAMA RASHIDA. You listen to me! From now on, you must behave yourself. Understand? Come now . . . up!
[MAMA RASHIDA *tugs at* SIKIRA *who is sprawling with sloppy nonchalance on the settee.*]
Up I say . . . into the kitchen . . . quick!
SIKIRA [*in feigned English accent which comes out in the desperate stammer of a he-goat just before coitus*]. Why . . . oo-o-h, my d-a-r-ling, dhe M-a-m-a of R-r-r-a-a-s-h-ida-a, w-h-y! Don't you want us to do like Americans in the cinema?
[*She kisses* MAMA RASHIDA *on the cheek*]
MAMA RASHIDA [*roughly, pulling her up*]. Go prepare food . . . do something – anything, I beg of you . . . yam is on fire . . . pound it . . . anything . . . just go!
[*She succeeds in hustling* SIKIRA *out toward the kitchen.*]

SCENE III

We are faced with an exquisite slice of feminine beauty: LIZA. *Her dress is one of the latest in* vogue, *but tastefully chosen in colour, design and cut. She 'click-clacks' neatly on high-heels onto the threshold, then through the opened front door into the living-room, stops, taken aback by the domestic impression: antiquated walls, cushions here, a couple of drink-stools upturned over there, political posters everywhere, an old matchet dangling warningly up there, a rifle minding its own business over here – all told, a curiously uncensored picture of well-meaning chaos.*

Absorbing the initial impact of this disarray, LIZA *steps farther into the living-room, trying hard to maintain her aplomb: the erect, self-assured bearing of a young banana plant. She goes from one poster to another, scanning the loud-mouthed slogans, and appraising the house generally. From the direction of the kitchen, the purposeful pounding of yams in a mortar explodes, briefly distracting* LIZA'S *attention. She soon identifies both sound and purpose ... and resumes her scrutiny.*

Presently MAMA RASHIDA *bustles in from the kitchen, about to blow her smoke-harassed nose into the raised lower tip of her wrapper. Halts, seeing* LIZA *who is still fascinated by the posters.* MAMA RASHIDA *stands transfixed, unnerved, utterly dumbfounded with shame at the topsy-turvy rascality in the living-room. Perhaps, it is not too late to do something about it ... Stealthily* MAMA RASHIDA *sidles to where the stack of cushions is. Eyes watching* LIZA, *she reaches, or rather feels for a couple of cushions, brings these down from the crude pile, sets them on a chair, then starts lifting the chair to position it properly; but the bottom-support of the chair unhinges, causing the body-work to fall apart. A loud pained crash results, followed quickly by a querulous clatter of falling lumber pieces.*

LIZA *turns round swiftly with a start;* MAMA RASHIDA *goes into a freeze, stubbornly holding on to the ridiculous remains of the broken chair, and looking defiantly stupid.*

For a while, they both stare silently at each other – LIZA *questioning, apologetic;* MAMA RASHIDA *tense, defensive – a rain-soaked old bird trapped in the corner of a small room, hopeless, waiting for the inevitable grip of a captor!*

At last, LIZA *ventures to speak.*

LIZA. Hel ... hello!

[*no response.*]

I . . . how d'you do? . . . Er . . . the master . . . to the airport? Boy . . .

[*mingling gestures with words*]

The boy . . . carry my load . . . he told me master went with friend to airport . . . to meet . . . me . . . to meet . . . airport.

MAMA RASHIDA [*sepulchrally*]. We . . . we did not know that you would come so . . . so early!

LIZA. Oh . . . I'm sorry.

[*She takes disintegrated chair from* MAMA RASHIDA *and starts fixing the parts together.*]

Our plane arrived ahead of schedule. We were going to stop in Liberia and Ghana, but the weather was atrocious, so we flew direct to Lagos.

MAMA RASHIDA [*not getting the meaning of "atrocious"*]. Hunh?

LIZA. I beg your pardon?

MAMA RASHIDA. You say . . . the weather?

LIZA. Oh, atrocious – I mean . . . bad. Not good . . . you know? Not clear . . . weather . . . dark . . . cloud . . . black. Like smoke in kitchen . . .

[*She laughs realising* MAMA RASHIDA *too is beginning to dare a smile.*]

MAMA RASHIDA. Ahennnn. [*She laughs now, feeling more relaxed.*]

[SIKIRA *tears in from the kitchen, fixes her gaze to the floor, and with self-pitying unconcern, grunts, as though addressing the bare floor whose business it should be to bounce off the message to the listening women.*]

SIKIRA. I want to say something, o!

[LIZA *and* MAMA RASHIDA *stop laughing and look at her.*]

The yam – you asked me to pound the yam; I have pounded the yam o!

MAMA RASHIDA. That is good. Now hurry and warm up the stew.

[SIKIRA *now raises her gaze, bears it down on* LIZA *– an acid, biting through* LIZA. MAMA RASHIDA *secretly gestures* SIKIRA *to leave.* SIKIRA *turns slowly, and goes back into the kitchen, sulking.* LIZA, *baffled by her attitude looks in her direction then turns to* MAMA RASHIDA *for some explanation.* POLYCARP *appears from rear-rooms.*]

MAMA RASHIDA. Oh, Polycarp . . . take this [*giving him money*]. Get a taxi quick, go to airport, tell Master sister Liza is here already.

[POLYCARP *runs off.*]

Sister, come with me to your room.

LIZA. Surely.

MAMA RASHIDA [*leading the way toward ante-rooms*]. Freedom is under your bed but he won't . . .

LIZA. What is?

MAMA RASHIDA. Freedom.

LIZA [*puzzled*]. Freedom?

MAMA RASHIDA. The master's snake.

LIZA [*stopping short*]. The master's what?

MAMA RASHIDA. His snake . . . for Politics.

LIZA. Under *my* bed?

MAMA RASHIDA. He won't trouble you. Freedom is the master's goodluck snake.

LIZA. Isn't that sweet!

MAMA RASHIDA. Whenever he goes to campaign, master takes Freedom with him and wraps him round his arm like a gold bangle.

LIZA. Most . . . spectacular! But . . . please, do me a favour . . . get it out of my room.

MAMA RASHIDA. Oh, but it is also the master's room, and breeze blows into it more than any other room.

LIZA. What has that got to do with it?

MAMA RASHIDA. The master says Freedom likes breeze, so he put him in that room.

LIZA. Listen, Mama, do me a favour, get someone to . . .
  [*Urgently.*]
  Where's that boy?

MAMA RASHIDA. Who? Polycarp?

LIZA [*calling*]. Poo-ly-ca-a-r-rp!

MAMA RASHIDA. We sent him to the airport – you forget?

LIZA. Well then, get the kitchen-maid [*indicating kitchen*] in there to do it!

MAMA RASHIDA [*sheepishly*]. Who? You mean . . . Sikira?

LIZA [*calling*]. Sikira!
  [*No answer.*]
  S-i-k-i-r-a!

SIKIRA [*calling from offstage*]. What is it, o?

LIZA. Come here, quick!
  [SIKIRA *comes, wielding a soup ladle. Dowdily clad in her work-a-day clothes, shoeless and without her veil on, she is the very model of a meritorious kitchen maiden.*]

SIKIRA [*straight-faced*]. Who called Sikira, o?

22

LIZA [*coaxingly*]. Sikira, honey, I've been on the plane for over ten hours. Just sitting ... you know ... one gets tired. Naturally, I need a rest.

SIKIRA [*nonchalantly licking sauce on ladle with her tongue, and at the same time noisily sucking in air to balm the pepper-scorched tongue*]. So?

LIZA. Get that snake out of my room, will you, please?

SIKIRA. Me! Without the master telling me to? K'abo!*

[LIZA *studies the two women briefly and decides that further dialogue with them would be fruitless.*]

LIZA. Very well then ... we'll have to just sit down, fold our arms, and wait patiently for the master ... won't we?

MAMA RASHIDA [*to* SIKIRA]. I was trying to tell Sisi Liza how much the master loves that snake ...

SIKIRA. Ah, that one na 'tory leke plasas!*

MAMA RASHIDA. Also, how the master always takes Freedom with him whenever he goes to campaign for politics all around the ...

SIKIRA [*with gossipy interest*]. Ah! Politics ... that one na *ogongo*!*

[*Makes a sweeping cross farther into the living-room and blabs to* LIZA.]

Not only is the master in love ... madly in love with Politics, he breathes Politics, he washes his mouth every morning with Politics, he sleeps with Politics and dreams of ...

[*Becoming quite demonstrative.*]

At night, deep in the middle of the night, the master grabs his pillow in his sleep ... holds it high above his head like a flag ...

[SIKIRA *holds spoon above her head.*]

... and he sings:

Freedom, Freedom
Everywhere there must be freedom,
Freedom for ...

LIZA. Is that so?

SIKIRA. In bed ... terrible ... you wait; you'll see him tonight.

[*Sings*]

Freedom for ...

You don't even have to keep awake to see. The master's voice will wake you up!

[*giggles naughtily*]

MAMA RASHIDA. Sikira!

LIZA [*cooly caustic.*] Someone ought to have told you, my dear girl, that it isn't proper for a *housemaid* to go peeping into the bedroom of her master at night or at any other . . .

[MAMA RASHIDA *and* SIKIRA *exchange glances. To them,* LIZA *must be one thing – out of her mind.*]

SIKIRA. Housemaid!

[*Incensed, to* MAMA RASHIDA.]

Did you hear that grasshopper? I told you she would come and kick everybody round and round . . .

LIZA. What did you say?

SIKIRA. Oohhoo!

[*Girds her wrapper tightly, ready for a fight.*]

Come on! You say you are a doctor? I will show you who I am!

[*Feigns a charge at* LIZA.]

[MAMA RASHIDA *hurries over, and intercepts* SIKIRA. *They struggle.*]

MAMA RASHIDA. Patience, you, patience, I say . . .

SIKIRA. Let go, Mama Rashida! that fowl wants her proud feathers plucked!

LIZA [*rising*]. Now wait a minute!

MAMA RASHIDA. Calm down!

SIKIRA. I'd rather die than let that cockroach kick *me* around!

MAMA RASHIDA. I said calm . . .

LIZA. Who is a cockroach?

SIKIRA. Who is a housemaid?

MAMA RASHIDA [*pinioning* SIKIRA'S *arms behind her*]. Now you . . . calm that hot temper right now, or I'll hit you!

SIKIRA. Didn't you hear what that antelope called *me*?

LIZA. I'm sorry, there must be a . . .

MAMA RASHIDA. Listen to that, she says she's sorry.

SIKIRA. I don't want to hear . . .

MAMA RASHIDA [*whacking* SIKIRA'S *arm*]. Quiet! Ta-ta-ta-ta-ta-ta! What has got into you?

SIKIRA. First thing that mosquito did was land on my head, biting me all over the . . .

MAMA RASHIDA. All right, that's enough – listen to what she has to say, now, will you? Abah!

[*With the self-assured calm of a sophisticate who wouldn't be lured into any form of female caterwauling,* LIZA *stands a couple of feet away from the other two.*]

LIZA. Maybe I'm . . . getting everybody . . . confused or something. Is this Mr Lejoka-Brown's house? By that I mean: the house of Mr Rahman Lejoka-Brown?

MAMA RASHIDA. This is Mr Rahman Lejoka-Brown's house, sister – the same that once housed his forebears...
 [*Rubbing her hands together prayerfully.*]
May Allah the All-Powerful, the All-Seeing, protect it from the hands of Destroyers and from the eyes of Witchcraft and from the...

LIZA [*impatiently*]. Sure, sure, sure... Now that that's established, let's turn to the next point. My dear women, six years ago, Mr Lejoka-Brown – er... Rahman Lejoka-Brown, that is... Mr Rahman Lejoka-Brown and I, got married.

SIKIRA [*a grunt*]. Halleluya!

LIZA. In Court...
 [*Holding out her ringed finger.*] ... ring and all.

SIKIRA. Ehen? Therefore!
 [*Singing to the tune of Bobby Benson's* Taxi Driver *highlife.**]
If you marry in Magistrate Court nko?
I don't care
If you marry in American Toronto!
I don't care
Whether you wear all rings in this world o,
I don't care
Whether you know book *tele** you tire o,
I don't care!

MAMA RASHIDA. Sikira!

SIKIRA. I've slept more nights with the master than you have, therefore...

LIZA. More wh-at?

SIKIRA. More nights; therefore, by native law and custom, I hold a senior place in this house.

MAMA RASHIDA. Enough! Come now!
 [*Shoves* SIKIRA *roughly out of the living-room.*]
To your room!

LIZA [*blankly*]. Native law and what!

SIKIRA [*over her shoulder*]. Whether you like it or not!

MAMA RASHIDA. Out!
 [*Escorts* SIKIRA *from the room.*]
 [LIZA, *alone in the living-room, stares absently in front of her, absorbing the shock.*

Soon MAMA RASHIDA *re-enters. She stops short at the door, and contemplates* LIZA *from that distance, wondering whether to approach her. At last, she goes up to* LIZA, *scans her over again briefly, then speaks.*]

MAMA RASHIDA. Didn't you know? Didn't the master tell you?
[*No answer.*]
That is very bad. Poor child. You are not alone in this house.

LIZA. Where are my things?

MAMA RASHIDA. Things?

LIZA. My things, Mama – suitcases . . . everything.

MAMA RASHIDA. Oh, . . . Polycarp put them in your room.

LIZA [*rising*]. Get me a taxi, would you please?

MAMA RASHIDA. Taxi! It is not easy to get a taxi here, Sister. One will have to go to Idumagbo bus stop to . . .

LIZA. Well . . . phone one, please, phone . . .

MAMA RASHIDA. Phone? What is phone?
[LIZA *gapes at her, dumbfounded.*]

LIZA [*heading for rear rooms*]. What room are my things in?

MAMA RASHIDA. The last one.
[LIZA *steps out. Freezes. Her back is still visible to the audience. She has just remembered something. Slowly, she turns round, her right hand clasped over her forehead as if stricken with a severe headache, and totters back into the living-room.*]

LIZA. Hail Mary, Mother of God . . . help me out of this zoo!
[*She flops dejectedly into a chair.*]

MAMA RASHIDA [*kneeling beside* LIZA]. Sister, I beg of you . . . do not let anger turn your head inside out. Have patience, I pray you. Come . . . come with me to the kitchen and get some salt and pepper in your stomach.
[*Extends her hand to* LIZA.]
Come, Sister . . . you can think things over while you are eating.

LIZA. Think things over! Oooh no. There's nothing . . . totally, clearly, absolutely . . . [*Hysterically.*] . . . nothing to think over, Mama. I cannot . . . repeat: cannot, I cannot and will never surrender my person to be devoured in this . . . blatantly decadent, third-rate domestic circus! Nor will I ever condescend to sharing the same monster of a husband with that . . . that . . .

[*Points toward rear-rooms after* SIKIRA.]

... that smutty, ill-bred, foul-mouthed, uncouth, mangy, grossly ribald, whipper-snapper of a chipmunk!

MAMA RASHIDA [*mild protest*]. Now, now, the master is not a monster!

LIZA. I don't care what he ...

[*Stops abruptly for a full appraisal of* MAMA RASHIDA.]

Who are you, by the way?

MAMA RASHIDA. Who – me?

LIZA. Yes – you.

MAMA RASHIDA. Why? Didn't the master tell you that too?

LIZA. Forget the apologies, Mama. Just hand it to me straight!

MAMA RASHIDA. It is well then.

[*Kneels down prayerfully.*]

By the Grace of Allah, the All-Merciful, the All-Providing ...

LIZA [*disgusted*]. Fire and brimstone!

MAMA RASHIDA [*rising*]. Toh! I'm his first wife, o!

[*They stare at each other.*]

BLACKOUT

SCENE IV

Lights on forestage: Major LEJOKA-BROWN *and* OKONKWO *emerge from one side of the stage to sit in front of a panel indicating:* LAGOS INTERNATIONAL AIRPORT. *They are both eating oranges bought off the tray of a girl-hawker who kneels, customarily, to rive off the orange rinds – Nigerian style. With casual expertise,* LEJOKA-BROWN *spits out the pips direct into the girl's tray – again Nigerian style.*

OKONKWO [*with a quick glance at his wristwatch*]. The plane will be here anytime now, Major!

LEJOKA-BROWN. Are you there? The world has changed, brother. You know?

OKONKWO. How?

LEJOKA-BROWN. Here I am, running up and down, renting a flat, getting restless, going crazy! Just because ... I mean,

I whose grandfather had a hundred and fifteen wives, I tell you ... one hundred plus ten plus five breathing wives all at once under his very roof! But here I am, with only two little crickets, expecting one more – just one more canary, and I can't just pick her up by the arm and say to her: "Woman, I forgot to tell you; but as the Whiteman says, 'better late than never!' Here – meet your other ehm ... sisters-in-marriage!"

OKONKWO. If you dare do that, she'll make you shit in your trousers!

LEJOKA-BROWN [*taking offence*]. Who? Me, shit in my trousers? Now, that's taking it too far, mister! I mean – I don't pray to lose Liza, true – but, dammit, no woman can make *me* shit in my trousers, man!

OKONKWO. Just you wait!

LEJOKA-BROWN [*importantly*]. After all, let's face it, I got into all this mess in order to make her feel proud!

OKONKWO [*guffaws*]. That's a good one!

LEJOKA-BROWN. You think I'm lying?

OKONKWO. Oh no – tell her that, she'll like it!

[*A Shoeblack breezes in, carrying his kit and calling out for clients: "shine!" LEJOKA-BROWN beckons him over and places a shod-foot on a thigh of the kneeling boy who starts polishing the shoe with exaggeratedly brisk competence.*]

LEJOKA-BROWN. Well, look – if I'd remained on my father's cocoa farm, I wouldn't have got my crazy head into Politics, see? And if I hadn't gone into politics, I wouldn't have got tangled up with these other women – at least, not with Sikira.

OKONKWO. So how would your Politics make Liza proud?

LEJOKA-BROWN. She's a woman ...

OKONKWO. And so?

LEJOKA-BROWN. Collecting degrees in medicine, ready to join Lejoka-Brown afterwards. Now, you tell me which is better:

[*Rises to demonstrate, Master-of-Ceremonies fashion.*]

"Ladies and Gentlemen, I have pleasure in introducing to you this evening, the Chairlady of this august occasion..." People clap – pra-pra-pra-pra-pra ... "She is the one and only Dr Mrs Elizabeth Lejoka-Brown, MD, MSc, wife of ..

[*Drops his voice.*]

... an Ijebu-Ijesha cocoa farmer!" Now listen to this:
[*More robust voice.*]
"... She is the one and only Dr the Honourable Mrs. Elizabeth Lejoka-Brown, MD (Yale), MSc (Gynaecology), wife of the one and only Federal Government Minister of Agriculture and Housing, Mister the Honourable Major Rahman Taslim Akinjide Lejoka-Brown, ON*, MHR*, Esquire!" A man must measure up, brother.
[*Tosses a coin at Shoeblack who catches it deftly in mid-air, bows smartly and exits.*]

OKONKWO. If I were you, Major, I'd go easy with Liza, at least, till the elections are over; treat her like an egg.
[*Lights a cigarette.*]
A paddler doesn't say a crocodile has an ugly lump on its snout, until he has safely crossed the river!

LEJOKA-BROWN. You mean I shouldn't tell her all that?

OKONKWO. You can tell her if you like. But don't just start talking blo-blo-blo-blo-blo... like an over-beaten war prisoner. No. Now, this is where the *Egg Treatment* comes in. You sit beside her. Then you take her hand... gently. Like so...
[*Takes orange-hawker's hand, and starts demonstrating.*]
It is an egg, Major, and you must handle it with care, lest it break! You start kissing it... like so...
[*Simulates kissing action, while girl stares blankly about, baffled.*]
Gently, tenderly... you go up, up... until you reach her neck. You stop there for a while, kissing one spot again and again, while you're talking.

POLYCARP [*calling from offstage*]. Major!

LEJOKA-BROWN. Someone calling?
[*They look about.*]

OKONKWO. No – nobody...
[*Continues.*]
Next thing, you're blowing cool air on her ear. Gently... like a rat. Then... you bite her ear-lobe. Again, gently. Mind you, you don't kiss it.

POLYCARP [*Louder but still offstage*]. Major!

OKONKWO. Ear-lobes aren't meant to be kissed. Know what I mean? You bite it – with your lips, of course...
[*Throws coin into girl's tray. Girl lifts her tray and hurries off, as we hear the roar of a Boeing 707 jet landing.*]

OKONKWO. That must be her plane now!
[*They start moving off.*]
POLYCARP [*louder*]. Major!
[*Polycarp bursts in urgently, panting.*]
POLYCARP. Beg to report sah!
[*The men turn, facing him.*]
Di '*yawo* done come for house, sah!
LEJOKA-BROWN. Hunh?
POLYCARP. Di madam – from America.
OKONKWO. Come where?
LEJOKA-BROWN [*masking his fright*]. Are you listening to the crazy idiot?
[*Threatens to strike* POLYCARP.]
When did I become your joke-mate?
POLYCARP. Na true Oga Major – I no craze yet.
LEJOKA-BROWN. But she said 5 o'clock!
OKONKWO. Maybe her plane arrived ahead of schedule.
LEJOKA-BROWN [*to* POLYCARP]. You mean she has entered our house ... on ... her own two feet?
POLYCARP. I swear, master, make God hammer me for head if say na lie I ...
LEJOKA-BROWN. Lai la!*
OKONKWO. And she saw ... the other women?
POLYCARP. Sah?
LEJOKA-BROWN. Liza take eye see Mama Rashida?
POLYCARP. Yes, Major, she see Mama Rashida well-well.
LEJOKA-BROWN. What about Sikira?
POLYCARP. She see 'am *gaan** – dem two.
[*Slowly, speechlessly,* LEJOKA-BROWN *begins to sink down, absently, ending up in a vulgar squat – the way one does over a pit toilet.* OKONKWO *watches him curiously then beckons to* POLYCARP.]
OKONKWO [*with impish delight*]. Here boy.
[*Hands* POLYCARP *a coin.*]
Looks like your master needs toilet paper!
[POLYCARP *stands confused.*]
Hurry, go buy some!
[POLYCARP *takes off.*]
LEJOKA-BROWN [*peremptorily*]. Hey! What's the matter? Hunh?
[POLYCARP *halts.*]
Madman, where are you going?

30

POLYCARP. I dey go buy toilet paper sah.
LEJOKA-BROWN. I see ... for who?
POLYCARP [*respectfully*]. For you sah.
LEJOKA-BROWN. Ehen? I see ... Na so your papa dey take shit? Hunh? Answer. When your Papa wan go latrine, he go take shokoto put for *nyash**; he carry damask agbada cover body, take cap knock for head finish, then he come *butu** dey shit for International Airport?
POLYCARP. Sorry sah!

[LEJOKA-BROWN *casts a malevolent glance in the direction of* OKONKWO *who is rolling on the bench, delirious with laughter over his friend's discomfiture.*]

LEJOKA-BROWN. Did Mama Rashida and Sikira make introduction to Liza?
POLYCARP. I no know, Major.
LEJOKA-BROWN. Did Liza ask Mama Rashida and Sikira who dem be?
POLYCARP. I no know, Major.
LEJOKA-BROWN. Well then, did Mama Rashida and Sikira say anything to Liza? Anything at all?
POLYCARP. I no know, Major.
LEJOKA-BROWN [*hotly, springing to his feet and seizing* POLYCARP *by the scruff of the neck*]. Don't "Major" me, you goat! What are you good for, anyway? *This* you don't know; *that*, you don't – what are you? A banana? Don't you have ears? Or you mean to tell me that Mama Rashida and Sikira became dumb all of a sudden and didn't say one word to Liza? Not one word that you heard?
POLYCARP. Oh, dem spoke, Oga Major.
LEJOKA-BROWN. What, Oga Idiot? Spoke what? Angrily? ... Laughingly?
POLYCARP. Sisi Liza enter for di house ...

[LEJOKA-BROWN *bends down to listen keenly;* OKONKWO *also leans over.*]

I help Sisi Liza tote her load go inside house. Mama Rashida and Sikira dem dey inside parlour by dat time.
LEJOKA-BROWN. Ehen?
POLYCARP. Den Sisi Liza look Mama Rashida for face and tell Mama Rashida say ...
OKONKWO. What?

POLYCARP. "Please send somebody to go call master."
LEJOKA-BROWN. And?
POLYCARP [*vacantly*]. So, I run four-forty* come, sah.
LEJOKA-BROWN. That's all, hunh?
POLYCARP. Tory* finish, sah.
OKONKWO. Poly-Poly!
POLYCARP [*naively appreciative*]. God dey, Oga.
LEJOKA-BROWN [*to* OKONKWO]. You see di kpokpo-gari* way God gimme for houseboy?

[LEJOKA-BROWN *lurches at* POLYCARP *who dodges a kick and runs off, chased by his master, agbada billowing in the wind.* OKONKWO *runs after them.*]

FADE OUT

SCENE V

Back at LEJOKA-BROWN'S *home.* MAMA RASHIDA *and* LIZA *are deep in conversation.*

MAMA RASHIDA. But then again, Sister, four years for man without a woman is not small matter.
LIZA. Granted ... but to go so far as to marry other women and to keep lying to me in his letters that I was the only woman in the world he – ugh!
MAMA RASHIDA. Oh, but it is true. You are the only woman that the master really cares for.
LIZA. For Heaven's sake – stop defending the devil!
MAMA RASHIDA. I'm not defending ...

[*Goes up to her, and whispers.*]

The master – he married Sikira simply for politics. Her mother – Sikira's mother, is the President of our Union, and in order to ...
LIZA. Union?
MAMA RASHIDA. All women who sell in market have a big Union.
LIZA. How nice.

MAMA RASHIDA. Sometimes I ... Hunh? "Nice", you say? Oooh no, Sister. You mistake. If I tell you my trouble in trade now, you will cry blood for me. You wait ...

[MAMA RASHIDA *hurries out. Curious,* LIZA *starts tiptoeing toward rear door to take a peep at what* MAMA RASHIDA *is up to. In that instant,* MAMA RASHIDA *bursts in carrying a basket cage of live chickens. She collides harshly with* LIZA, *jolting the chickens into a protest of mass squawking, and frightening* LIZA *in the extreme.*]

MAMA RASHIDA. Time was, Sister, when chicken was "nice trade". But now! Every lizard of a petty-trader has climbed up to sell chickens. So what happens? Chickens price climbs up. Nobody buys.

[*Reaches for a chicken.*]

This one I bought in village – five shillings! Now I can't even sell in city market for seven-and-six. I ask you: is that "*nice*" trade?

[*Car hums to a stop outside.*]

Last week, I bought fifty-three fowls in village, you know how much I ...

[*Cocks her head – listening.*]

I think the master – they come now.

LIZA [*hurrying to window*]. You leave us alone awhile, will you?

MAMA RASHIDA [*lifting her basket, and backing away*]. I ... beg you ... do not fight ...

[*Exits.*]

[LEJOKA-BROWN *and* OKONKWO *approach house.* POLYCARP *is behind them.* LIZA *catches a glimpse of them through the window, then retreats quickly to sit on settee.*]

LEJOKA-BROWN [*to* OKONKWO]. Are you there? The "Egg Treatment" won't work now.

OKONKWO. I doubt it, Major.

LEJOKA-BROWN. Goat!

POLYCARP. Sir!

LEJOKA-BROWN. Run on ... tell them we're coming.

POLYCARP. Yes, Major.

[*He hurries into house.*]

OKONKWO [*to a feet-dragging* LEJOKA-BROWN]. Don't waste time, Major.

[OKONKWO *shoves him toward the threshold,* LEJOKA-BROWN *glues an ear to the door, listens in, then stands erect, crossing himself, and turning away.*]

LEJOKA-BROWN [*weightily*]. Trouble catch monkey, monkey chop pepper!
[*Crosses himself again.*]
OKONKWO. Aha! I thought you were a Muslim.
LEJOKA-BROWN [*indicating* LIZA *within*]. Catholic!
[LEJOKA-BROWN *composes himself, then timidly eases door open. Sees* LIZA; *a moment of awkward silence.* LEJOKA-BROWN *and* LIZA *staring blankly at each other. Then summoning up courage,* LEJOKA-BROWN *throws his arms up in exaggerated declamation, and croons expansively.*]
For she's a jolly good fellow
Yes, she's a jolly good fellow
She's a jolly good f-e-l . . .
[*Arms outspread in readiness for an embrace,* LEJOKA-BROWN *now waddles with clumsy gaiety towards* LIZA, *to engulf her in a bear-hug.*]
. . . l-o-w!
LIZA [*coolly stopping him*]. No . . . please!
LEJOKA-BROWN [*persistent*]. Welcome, darling, no ceremonies, we've missed –
LIZA [*still resisting*]. Not now, please – I have . . . a pain!
LEJOKA-BROWN. Pain?
LIZA. Yes, a pain. In my back: an excruciatingly acute sacro-iliac muscle spasm.
[LEJOKA-BROWN's *arms slide down* LIZA's *body involuntarily.*]
LEJOKA-BROWN. I . . . I don't know what that means, but . . .
[*Covering up his chagrin.*]
It must be from sitting in that crazy aeroplane for so long. Anyway, welcome all the same – oh . . .
[*Looks about him.*]
I want you to meet my . . . are you there . . .
[*To* OKONKWO *who is standing at a respectful distance.*]
Come over here, you rascal.
[OKONKWO *comes forward.*]
Lawyer G A Okonkwo! Gideon Abednego Okonkwo Esquire.
[OKONKWO *bows gallantly.*]
What is that? Come on . . . shake her hand like a man, my friend!
[OKONKWO *holds out a hand uncertainly;* LIZA *takes it courteously, but without a smile.* LEJOKA-BROWN *feels somewhat relieved.*]

Aha! Now, Wife, you'd better make the best of that handshake. Why, the hand you're holding now, belongs to the future Attorney General of this Federation after the elections.
OKONKWO [*jokingly*]. Not Chief Justice?
LEJOKA-BROWN. No – Attorney General. That's a sound with power, Man: Attorney General! Sounds like: Major General! But: Chief Justice? What is in Chief Justice? I mean – any village chief can do Justice. Oya – shake her hand again ... Di Attorn-e-y General!

[LIZA *favours* OKONKWO *with a wry smile, then withdraws her hand. Patting* OKONKWO *proudly on the shoulder,* LEJOKA-BROWN *continues.*]

Now, Wife, you think this man looks like a retired choirmaster Ohhh ... you should have seen him in the Congo. Shoulder to shoulder we fought back those long-nosed Belgian mercenaries for five and half days without food, without water, until the ...

[*Sings with nostalgic gusto.*]

Ai re-m-e-m-b-a-h
When I was a soljar ...

[*To* LIZA *who has turned away.*]

Hey, what's the matter?

OKONKWO [*trying to lighten things up*]. Come now, Major, let's celebrate, bring drinks, at least, let me enjoy some of the fringe benefits of my acquaintance with Liza!

LEJOKA-BROWN. Of course let's – [*suddenly curious*]. Fringe benefit – what's that?

OKONKWO. Oh, it means "little, little, extra pleasures" – sort of ...

LEJOKA-BROWN. Oh ... yes ... why not ...

[*Nervously flippant as he heads toward kitchen area.*]

Drinks, everybody. Let's celebrate. Where is everybody?

LIZA. I beg your pardon!

LEJOKA-BROWN [*freezing*]. Hunh?

LIZA. What "Everybody" are you summoning, Mr Lejoka-Brown?

LEJOKA-BROWN [*evasively*]. Me?

LIZA. You are Mr Lejoka-Brown, aren't you?

LEJOKA-BROWN [*non-committally*]. By the Grace of God.

LIZA. Who, and who, and who then d'you mean by "everybody"!

LEJOKA-BROWN. You mean . . . ?
LIZA. Don't you know what I mean?
LEJOKA-BROWN. Oh, I mean . . . emm . . . people . . . emm . . . dependants . . . you know . . . people of the house . . . emm . . . extended family . . . you know: citizens.
LIZA. What kind of citizens?
LEJOKA-BROWN. Hunh?
LIZA. I said what kind of citizens Mr Lejoka-Brown?
LEJOKA-BROWN. Oh . . . women . . . women . . . emm . . . like you . . .
[*Wildly waving his hands in a vain attempt to think up a less incriminating description.*]
Women . . . women . . . women, women . . . emm . . . you know what I mean?
LIZA. Market women?
LEJOKA-BROWN. Hunh?
LIZA. Well, when you went: "Women, women, women", I couldn't help picturing a crowd of market women, with the President of the Market Women's Union, her well-mannered daughter, and also . . . a loyal member of that Union who could be selling chickens.
[LEJOKA-BROWN, *stunned, deflated, stares vacantly at* LIZA *then at* OKONKWO *and back at* LIZA *as he manages to stammer.*]
LEJOKA-BROWN. So . . . you . . . emm . . . I . . . I take it then that . . . emm . . . emm . . . things have gone well between you and them . . .
[*Indicates rear of house.*]
LIZA. Things? What things?
LEJOKA-BROWN. Hunh? Oh, I mean . . . emm . . . things, things . . . emm . . . introduction ceremony et cetera.
LIZA. Oh, of course, I could hardly wait for that!
[LEJOKA-BROWN, *puzzled, hurries up to* OKONKWO *who turns his attention to a poster on the wall – not wanting to get involved.*]
LEJOKA-BROWN [*turning back to* LIZA]. And . . . you're not . . . angry?
LIZA. Angry! Why should I be?
[LEJOKA-BROWN *studies her briefly again, takes a deep breath, and goes to sit beside her.*]
LEJOKA-BROWN. All right, 'Lizabeth. I'll explain everything – from the beginning to Amen, and get it over.
LIZA [*feigning a smile*]. No. Never mind.

LEJOKA-BROWN. What?

LIZA. No need.

[LEJOKA-BROWN *lets out a loud guffaw of relief, misjudging* LIZA's *outward aura of levity, crosses excitedly over to* OKONKWO.]

LEJOKA-BROWN [*clamping a hand on* OKONKWO's *shoulder*]. What did I tell you? Now that's an African woman, truc-truc. You see? She ... she understands a man's need for certain ... emm ... "fringe benefits" of life! Come now – drinks, everybody. Let us celebrate.

LIZA. None for me, thank you.

OKONKWO. Aahh ... never mind, Major. Maybe Liza wants a quiet afternoon with you alone. We'll drink tomorrow evening.

LEJOKA-BROWN. All right, all right – tomorrow.

OKONKWO. Nice to have met you.

LIZA. Goodbye.

OKONKWO [*secretly tugging at* LEJOKA-BROWN's *garment as he passes by him toward the door*]. See me off a little, Major.

[LEJOKA-BROWN *and* OKONKWO *step outside, shut the door behind them.* OKONKWO *in a whisper to* LEJOKA-BROWN ...]

Don't be deceived, brother: she is boiling inside, never mind her ice-water calm.

[LEJOKA-BROWN *nods glumly.*]

Remember – the egg treatment. It might work now that she's sitting.

LEJOKA-BROWN. No, no, don't go away. Stay close by, I might need you, in case she starts tearing me up!

[LEJOKA-BROWN *shoves* OKONKWO *into a corner outside and re-enters living-room – a toothy, Cheshire-cat grin parting his lips.*]

So, ... how d'you like my house?

LIZA. It's divine!

LEJOKA-BROWN. Hunh? Well, it is a bit old – true. But as you say: it is ... emm ... divination-like. This house was built by my grandfather, one of the greatest warriors under Gbogungboro Ogedengbe of Ijeshaland! Have you heard of Kiriji war? Look at this.

[*Strides to wall, and unsheathes matchet.*]

With this, my grandfather plucked down fifty-three human heads in one battle. Out there ...

[*Points out into the back yard.*]

... in that big tomb, my grandfather and my father lie buried
... the peace of Allah on their spirits.
[*Sentimentally.*]
It is a *shrine* – this place. That's why I'm doing all I can, Liza, to preserve it.
[*Plants himself beside* LIZA, *his hand sneaking toward her own.*]
Why, a house like this **is** sacred, Wife. The spirits of our fathers dwell in it, they breathe in it.
[*He ogles critically at* LIZA'S *bosom.*]
Isn't this dress a little too low around your ... er ... shoulders?
[*She does not answer; he clasps a hand consolingly on hers.*]
Well, anyway, as time goes on you'll start dressing properly again. I know, it takes time to change back to African ways after being away in Whiteman's country so long.
[LEJOKA-BROWN *bends over and starts kissing* LIZA'S *hand – slowly but surely escalating the act along the length of her arm to the shoulder, then her neck, and finally her ear-lobe: à la "egg treatment". All the while, he is talking.*]
I'll become the Minister of Agric and Housing, Wife. By so, I will decide what houses to pull down and what *shrines* to leave alone ... and so on, and so on. Oh, I could become Prime Minister, too. Except ... people will say I want to be everything.
[*Blows air on* LIZA'S *ear.*]
As for you, Liza ...
[*Pecks at her ear-lobe.*]
... great plans! As soon as the elections are over, I'll build you a special, private hospital – all to yourself. I've saved up forty thousand pounds from my cocoa business for the ...
LIZA [*coolly*]. Mr Lejoka-Brown!
LEJOKA-BROWN. Hunh?
LIZA. Are you feeling hungry?
LEJOKA-BROWN [*amazed at the irrelevant suddenness of the question*]. Hungry? No.
LIZA. Then why, may I ask, were you eating my ear-lobe?
LEJOKA-BROWN. I wasn't *eating* your ear, Liza, I was kissing it.
LIZA. Well, sir, I am in no mood to be slobbered on!
[*Gets up and moves away: explosion any moment now.*]
LEJOKA-BROWN. Now listen to me, 'Lizabeth, I've been trying to welcome you ever since you ...

LIZA. No!
[*Whirls round, facing* LEJOKA-BROWN.]
You listen to me, Mr Major.
[*She advances, forcing* LEJOKA-BROWN *to back up defensively. They both look like awkward partners doing the tango.*]
Politician ... Rahman Taslim Lejoka-Brown!
[*His retreat is blocked by a chair.*]
I've been waiting patiently ... ooh, so patiently, for you to c-o-o-l it, so I could say something. But no. Now, you listen to me, buddy, and man, you listen good!
[*Kicks off her shoes.*]
Now, when *I* Elizabeth Tayanta, married *you* in the Congo, I had the impression that I was entering into a union with *you* alone, and you with *me*.

LEJOKA-BROWN. True, but ...

LIZA [*drowning his voice out*]. Never, Mr Lejoka-Brown, never did I once imagine that I was doomed to becoming one of your three sacrificial slaves in this ... this ...
[*With a sweeping gesture that takes in the entire house.*]
... nauseating, clay-walled, gas-chamber!

LEJOKA-BROWN [*hurt*]. Lai la i lan la!
[*Springs to his feet.*]
I won't have this house of my grandfather's insulted!

LIZA. Please, don't shout!

LEJOKA-BROWN. Get that straight!

LIZA. Your shouting will only succeed in attracting curious spectators from the outside, Mr Lejoka-Brown!

LEJOKA-BROWN. I don't care!

LIZA. Well I do! I hate washing my dirty underwear in public!

LEJOKA-BROWN. My dear woman, I'm not an underwear!

LIZA. Don't obscure the issue, please. It is quite apparent that a breach of faith has been flagrantly committed by you ...

LEJOKA-BROWN [*gruffly*]. As an African, I have a right to marry as many wives as I can handle ...

LIZA. Under native law and custom – true. But *our* marriage was performed in Court, Mr Lejoka-Brown! In the Congo: under the *French* law: one man, one woman. So ... don't you go around kidding yourself, fellow!

LEJOKA-BROWN. As a Muslim, I'm entitled to four, complete, live, breathing wives. No less.

LIZA. Ah-ah-ah-ah... that wasn't stipulated in our wedding agreement brother Rahman, was it?

LEJOKA-BROWN [*with a mumble of defeat*]. Don't lawyer me!

LIZA. Very well, then, let me make my final point. Since I hate sharing any personal possession with someone else...

LEJOKA-BROWN [*at top of his voice*]. I'm not a possession!

LIZA. Please, don't shout!

LEJOKA-BROWN. So, don't call me a possession, Lady! A-ha – am I a bag of cement? Or... or... do I look like a... a transistor radio? Or... or what do you think I am? A fifty by hundred plot of land on Ikorodu Road? A Volkswagen? Possession indeed!

LIZA. Only bushmen and hooligans shout.

LEJOKA-BROWN. Possession!

[LEJOKA-BROWN *crosses to window. He needs some fresh air.* LIZA *goes up to him.*]

LIZA. You must try to control your temper, Mr Lejoka-Brown. After all, remember, you'll soon be one of the leaders of a great African nation. Why then... you must learn to control your emotions.

[*Takes his hand, feeling his pulse.*]

Apart from the fact that wild displays of angry emotions can make you a social nuisance, you must realize the grave harm anger does to your health, Mr Lejoka-Brown. For instance... your pulse-rate now gives cause for alarm. Your adrenal glands, on top of your kidneys, are working themselves terribly hard. Your liver too is being badly affected; so are your nerves. What will happen next? Psychosomatic breakdown!

LEJOKA-BROWN [*pulling back, scared*]. Oohh... don't wish death on me, witch!

LIZA. Take your choice: peptic ulcer; high blood pressure; asthma; obesity; dermatitis; neuralgia; headache; insomnia; migraine; cardio-vascular...

LEJOKA-BROWN. Liza! Listen...

[*Makes earnest plea.*]

Sit... sit down...

[*Takes her arm in one hand, znd supporting her back with the other, he leads her toward settee.*]

Let's sit down like two real human beings, and I'll explain every...

LIZA [*spinning away from him*]. No. Not necessary.

LEJOKA-BROWN. Aahh...

[*Seizes her by the shoulders*].

'Lizabeth, you are angry, and I don't blame you. But listen... I beg you. I have enough headache with my politics as it is. Now, if you do anything to cause trouble at home and give me double, double, double headache – chuu!

[*Pauses, while* LIZA *considers*.]

You don't want my enemies to call me a bush pig, do you? "Bush pig Lejoka-Brown. He wants to be a national leader, yet his own house is *jagajaga** upside down!" Soon my political enemies will be singing:

[*Intones to the tune of the Nigerian National Anthem*.]

    Oh, people of Nigeria
    Why waste your precious votes
    On a bush pig like Lejoka-Brown
    Who wants to be premier?
    Can a pig with so much mess at home
    Clean up our nation's mess?

[*Pauses*.]

You want my enemies to call me a bush pig? I beg you, stay with me, have patience, and we shall solve this "palaver".

LIZA. On one condition –

LEJOKA-BROWN. Any condition Liza, anything you...

LIZA. Please, don't interrupt!

LEJOKA-BROWN. All right, talk.

[*Recoils to a chair, tamely*.]

LIZA. On this condition: you will regard me simply as a GUEST in this house while I plan how I can get out of this mess honourably.

LEJOKA-BROWN. A guest!

LIZA. You realize I know nobody in this country of yours to go to. So I pray you, bear with me till I make a final decision on what step to take next. During this period, I assure you that I shall mind my own business. And you, my dear fellow, you must...

LEJOKA-BROWN. Fellow!

LIZA. Like a good HOST, you must endeavour to mind your own business. If you dare meddle in my affairs, why then,

I will be constrained to take what might be an impetuous decision. In which case, you will have to bear full responsibility for the consequences of that impetuousness. OK?

LEJOKA-BROWN [*a growl*]. Consequences! Such as?

LIZA. Immediate divorce proceedings for one thing. You can't be that asinine. The grounds are ample and valid: breach of faith; extreme mental cruelty; incompatibility; adultery; gross negligence of...

LEJOKA-BROWN. Wait a minute, wait a minute! One at a time. First, this... "asinine" – what does *that* mean, divorce-law-wise?

LIZA. You never mind that for now. But do me a favour and remove that monster from under my bed, please!

LEJOKA-BROWN. What mons...? Oh, you mean Freedom? [*Amused.*]
Why, Freedom won't bite you. It's cooler for him in that...

LIZA. Please, let's not start a zoological seminar on the behavioural patterns of snakes! Thank you.

LEJOKA-BROWN. All right, o; Polycarp!

POLYCARP [*offstage*]. Beg to report, sah!

LEJOKA-BROWN. Make you take Freedom commot from under the bed, o!

POLYCARP [*still calling from offstage*]. Yes, sah.

[LIZA *exits into rear-rooms. Fanning himself with the bottom end of his jumper,* LEJOKA-BROWN *ambles out to meet* OKONKWO *on the porch.*]

OKONKWO. How now?

LEJOKA-BROWN. Bo, brother me, perspiration done make me sweat!

[*Sings to the tune of E T Mensah's "School Girl" highlife.*]
    Brother, I dey tell you,
    Booku woman no good o!

OKONKWO [*amused*]. Oh come on...

LEJOKA-BROWN.
    I say listen:
    University woman na wire o!*
    If you marry her,
    Trouble nahim go follow you:
    I dey tell you,
    Acada woman no good o.

OKONKWO. Is Liza staying?

LEJOKA-BROWN.
  I say listeni,
  B.A. Woman, make you run o!
  Brother listeni,
  Doctor woman, na katakata* o!
  If you marry her –
  Ugbarugba* na him go killi you
  I dey tell you...

Katakata dey come...
  [LIZA *approaches, carrying a transistor radio from which Handel's "Halleluyah Chorus" swells forth.* LEJOKA-BROWN *starts guiltily, converting his rendition into an ad lib.*] Oh, yes, the insurance policy make it comprehensive, and send in the bills...
  [OKONKWO *sneaks out of the porch and exits finally.* LEJOKA-BROWN *stands listening to the radio while* LIZA, *clad in shorts, gets busy sprinkling water on the bunch of clothes she is about to iron. Music stops and Announcer begins to introduce the time and signature tune for news of the hour.*]

LEJOKA-BROWN. Are you there...
  [*Jocularly.*]
What kind of music do you call that one? Alleluya, Alleluya, Alleluya – from Morning to Night: Alleluya, Alleluya!
  [*crosses to record-player.*]
One can't even walk to it, let alone dance to it. Listen... let me show you music. Real music.
  [*Picks up a record.*]
What is music, if it can't be danced to? Now listen to real music...
  [*Places the pick-up head on the record on player. Instantly, the brash sound of raw sakara music complete with the languid monotone of male solo, backed by a somnolent choral response, suffused with drums, "goje" and rattles, blasts forth, drowning the whole house.* LEJOKA-BROWN *capers in dance to the Sakara appeal, at the same time singing, wide-mouthed, along with the record.* LIZA *crosses over to the player and stops it.*]

LEJOKA-BROWN. A-ah! Why now?
  [*sober.*]
Listen, Liza...
  [*Steps toward* LIZA's *radio, clicks it off.*]

I swear, I'm going to do my best to treat you well in this house because no matter what, you are still my wife, and *I* will remain head. Hear me? I want peace in this house, true. But you can't set your separate rules and hand me an ultimatum. Oooh no, Woman. Two bulls can't drink from the same bucket at the same time: they will lock horns!

[LIZA *stands up defiantly, eyeball-to-eyeball with* LEJOKA-BROWN.]
LIZA. We shall see!

BLACKOUT

ACT 2

ACT 2

ACT 2

SCENE I

Three weeks later, in LEJOKA-BROWN'S *living-room.* LIZA, *in blouse and tight-fitting trousers, is sewing a dress on a portable machine.* SIKIRA *is sweeping loose pieces of cloth on the floor into a pile.* MAMA RASHIDA *is sitting on a sheepskin a little distance away. In front of her is a moderate-sized basket flanking which are two smaller ones. One by one,* MAMA RASHIDA *picks up the contents of the large basket – eggs – and with extreme delicacy, examines them against the light. Eggs that pass this ocular test go into the smaller basket on her right; addled failures are laid to rest in the basket to her left. She is, at the same time, listening to* LIZA. *Offstage, smithy work is going on: hammering, sawing, etc.*]

LIZA. Your next problem will be to create the *Demand*. And the best way to do this is...

MAMA RASHIDA. *Demand* is what again now? People who *sell*?

LIZA. No, no...that's *Supply*.

SIKIRA. Demand means people who go to market.

MAMA RASHIDA. Ah yes...

[LIZA *gestures* SIKIRA *towards her, and starts taking her measurements.*]

LIZA. You must lower your prices so more and more people can buy eggs.

MAMA RASHIDA [*Reciting*]. I lower my prices – for *Demand*.

LIZA. That's right. And with your chicken house now, you can make more eggs to sell than anybody else in your market.

MAMA RASHIDA. I shall have more eggs for *Supply*.

LIZA. E-x-actly!

[MAMA RASHIDA *swoops up to* LIZA *and embraces her gratefully, then kneels in prayer arms up-raised.*]

MAMA RASHIDA. Heey! My sister, may Allah grant you His blessing. May Allah fill your womb with children – plenty, plenty children until your *Supply* becomes greater than the *Demand*!

[LIZA, *flabbergasted, bursts out laughing.* SIKIRA *joins in; so does* MAMA RASHIDA *who has returned to the business with her eggs.*]

SIKIRA. Hm! You know, Sisi Liza, I was afraid when I heard you were coming from America, o!

LIZA. Why? You didn't even know who I was.

[*Proffers clothing to her.*]

Here – try this on . . .

[SIKIRA *holds out clothing at arm's length, admiring it. This is an undergarment.*]

SIKIRA. Well . . . they say when our African women go to England, or to America, or so-so-and-so, they come back wanting to be Headmasters, and kicking everybody round and round.

MAMA RASHIDA [*teasing*]. Now, now – don't feel too safe; Sisi Liza has been with us now only three weeks.

LIZA. That's right, Mama Rashida.

[*To* SIKIRA, *jocularly.*]

See? How do you know I won't kick you "round and round" like a headmaster yet!

[POLYCARP *bursts in shoulder-carrying a longish metal cage.*]

POLYCARP. Aunty Liza!

SIKIRA. Ugh!!

[*She freezes, her blouse half pulled up.* POLYCARP *looks away, embarrassed.*]

SIKIRA. Why you no dey let man know whenever you dey come sef?

POLYCARP. Whetin you want make I do? – Blow wisul?

[*Curses under his breath.*]

Jesus wept!

SIKIRA. Hm! Just like his master!

[*Hurries off to rear-rooms, to get dressed.*]

MAMA RASHIDA [*to* POLYCARP]. You done finish patapata?*

POLYCARP [*lowering cage onto floor*]. No ma – na wire done finish.

LIZA [*examining cage*]. How many have you done so far?

POLYCARP. Dis be eleven, ma. One more to finish, and den we fix di legs – nahim dat.

MAMA RASHIDA. Ehen! You and your over-sabi*! Which kin leg you want put again now?

POLYCARP. Na leg nahim go carry –

MAMA RASHIDA. No leg nothin'; you waste time, now go.

POLYCARP. Na true Mama Rashida – look . . .

[*Pulls out a booklet from a pocket.*]

Aunty Liza book talk say . . .

[*Reads laboriously from the book.*]

"Legs must ex . . . extend at least two feet from the ground to en . . . en . . . ens . . ."

LIZA. Ensure . . . to ensure free flow of air.

[*Rises, satisfied with the work.*]

Why, Polycarp, with such skill you should open up a Chicken House factory of your own.

MAMA RASHIDA. And sell our secret to the whole world? Ooh, no!

[*Gets money out from the inner recesses of her underskirt.*]

How much you want for more wire?

POLYCARP. Two pounds, ma. Five yards: eight shillings per one single every each yard.

MAMA RASHIDA [*shoving a small wad of money into his hand*]. Here ..

POLYCARP [*surprised*]. Two pounds ten?

MAMA RASHIDA. I dash you ten shilling for kola*!

POLYCARP. Hey! Thank you, Mama.

[*Heaves cage onto his shoulder and prances out gleefully.*]

MAMA RASHIDA [*to LIZA, who is back sewing*]. Sister, you put big ideas in Polycarp's head!

[*Enter SIKIRA in her new undergarment, looking quite natty, chic, sensually prim.*]

SIKIRA. Awu – Mama Rashida, your chicken house looks so good, I'm jealous, o!

[MAMA RASHIDA *resumes her chore.*]

LIZA [*to SIKIRA*]. Come over here.

[LIZA *scrutinizes the fitting of the undergarment – adjusting here, pinching there.*]

SIKIRA [*teasing*]. Can you imagine? In three months' time Mama Rashida will make so much profit from chicken eggs that the master will have enough money to borrow for his crazy politics.

[LIZA *hands her the dress she has just completed – a dainty, smartly cut artifice (about which the audience will know more later).*]

MAMA RASHIDA [*defiantly*]. Borrow my profits! To campaign politics? Allah forbid!

FADE OUT

SCENE II

Conference Room of the National Liberation Party, executive members settling down to the day's business. But first the usual social activity of light talk, and exchange of greetings normally preceding such occasions. We notice OKONKWO *in the background. A gavel is struck calling the house to order. Silence.*

OSAGIE. The Executive Committee of the National Liberation Party, meeting under the Chairmanship of Mr Rahman Lejoka-Brown will now begin its deliberations.

[*Bows to* LEJOKA-BROWN.]

Mr Chairman . . .

[*Sits and starts taking notes in the minutes file.*]

LEJOKA-BROWN. Gentlemen, our election campaign plans must follow a pattern of military strategy known as surprise and attack.\Now, what is: surprise and attack? Surprise and attack, Gentlemen, is "to catch the enemy off-guard, and wipe out his power before he can mobilize enough forces to launch a counter-attack." Are you there . . . now, how do we apply this strategy to our campaigns? Now listen . . . we shall concentrate our early campaigns on the outskirts . . .

[*Indicates on map with a cane.*]

In the villages . . . in the tiny fishing suburbs . . . and so on. Like a very busy husband who cannot afford a direct clash with a difficult wife, at the moment, we must steer clear of a face to face meeting with our political enemies in the big towns . . . we keep our hands off the cities. For the time being, mark you. For the time being. One rat at a time; you chase two, you miss both.

[*Mumbling ... whisperings: reactions by other members.*]

ONE MEMBER. S-i-l-e-n-c-e!

[*Quiet prevails again.*]

LEJOKA-BROWN. Now then. About one month before election day, we launch a sudden two-pronged drive from the small towns and villages right into the big towns and cities. Our political enemies are ... SURPRISED.

[*Clears his throat.*]

Then the ATTACK ...

[*More ardently.*]

From city to city, we run over the whole State with a heavy artillery of campaign speeches. And, brothers, by the time our enemies rally together to put up a resistance...

[*Throw his arms up.*]

... all over. We carry Ibadan ... Abeokuta falls under our feet ... we uproot Ilesha ... Oyo trembles into our open arms ... we welcome Ogbomosho ... Ilorin opens up the door, and we're in the north, Gentlemen. Once there, an arm of our propaganda brigade crosses over to Jos, Jos to Oturkpo, heading south ... Enugu puts up a tough fight, we hop over Enugu ... march through Port Harcourt ... sweep Calabar ... we begin campaigning in Onitsha ... cross over the bridge, dance through Asaba, shake up Benin, hop over to Warri and fullstop.

[*Dramatically mops the sweat from his brow with a handkerchief.*]

Well ... Gentlemen ... any query so far?

[*No answer.*]

Gentlemen, I said any que ...

[*Seven members pop up instantly, speaking simultaneously.*]

MEMBER 1. Mr President ...
MEMBER 2. Yes, question ...
MEMBER 3. I have the floor ...
MEMBER 4. Plenty ...
MEMBER 5. Just one ...
MEMBER 6. I want to know how ...
MEMBER 7. Of course ...

[*They all stop abruptly, and look at each other.*]

LEJOKA-BROWN [*playfully*]. Gentlemen, let's talk "one by each" please!

MEMBER 2 [*to* MEMBER 4]. Go ahead.
MEMBER 4 [*to* MEMBER 2, *politely*]. After you.
MEMBER 2 [*again to* MEMBER 4]. Do me a favour.
MALLAM GASKIYA. Aahhh ... [*furiously*]. Courtesy be damned! Now listen, Mr Chair ...
LEJOKA-BROWN [*striking gavel*]. I recognise Mr Osagie.
OSAGIE [*trying to be courteous*]. Mr Chairman ... er ... I ... I regret to say that I ... er ... I have some doubts as to ...
MALLAM GASKIYA. This is beyond doubts ... it's sheer ... Oh, hell ...
[*Rises again; hotly.*]
Now listen, everybody ...
A MEMBER. Mallam Gaskiya, you're out of order.
MALLAM GASKIYA. Protocol be hanged! Listen, fellows. Let's stop fooling ourselves. Please! This military Surprise and Attack nonsense just won't work in a political campaign.
ANOTHER MEMBER. Hear, hear!
[LEJOKA-BROWN *is rocking back and forth agitatedly in his chair, his eyes riveted acrimoniously on* MALLAM GASKIYA.]
MALLAM GASKIYA. And, aside from the fact that the present Leader of our Party is so old-fashioned and autocratic about the risky implementation of his whimsical strategy, this whole mumbo-jumbo about military exercise in a political set-up is a sham!
LEJOKA-BROWN [*rearing up*]. Now, you wait a min ...
[*Bedlam: everybody talking, nobody listening.* LEJOKA-BROWN's *voice, however, booms over the others.*]
LEJOKA-BROWN [*declaiming wildly*]. How do you know Surprise and Attack won't work in politics? What do you people know about politics – I mean hard-bone politics? Small, small boys, all of you ... went to Europe and America, studied book, came back, talk big talk. You think politics in book is politics in real life? You lie, Book-heads! Politics means action, and action means war. Therefore, Military Surprise and Attack can win us votes if only we ...
[MEMBERS *begin to walk out.*]
This is sabotage! Come back ... Mallam Gaskiya ... I said come back! Things must be done constitution-like. All right, all right, every jackass go home ... go ...
[*Tears map off board.*]
OKONKWO. Major!

LEJOKA-BROWN. What did I do wrong?

OKONKWO. The way you talked to them, know-what-I-mean? You seem to make them feel you want to order them around like in the army. This cannot work among people who are not in the army, Major.

LEJOKA-BROWN. Order them around! Ha! Me ... order them! What are you talking about?

[*Fiery.*]

It's *them* who are ordering me around. They think because I didn't go to America-Toronto or to England-Oxford as *they* did, that I am a bat with my head downwards. But they forget, they forget that even a bat, head-downwards, notices the way the birds fly. Oh, but you wait! Whether *they* like it or not, I'm going ahead with my Surprise and Attack plan for the campaigns.

[*Raises an arm Heavenwards.*]

And Allah help any crab among them who dares stop me!

[*Strides out, followed by* OKONKWO.]

I'll show them that I'm different ...

FADE OUT

SIKIRA [*as the lights come up on the other side of the stage*]. You're different.

SCENE III

LEJOKA-BROWN'S *living-room.* SIKIRA *is now wearing a tight-fitting, micro-mini snippet of a dress. Other attributes of this: a saucily low neckline exposing much of her back, and a sumptuous sweep of her "frontal undulations".* LIZA *is standing by, fitting the dress on* SIKIRA, *and fussing with one part of it and then the other.*

SIKIRA. You are a strong woman, with a strong, strong heart. Sometimes I wish I, too, had your kind of strong, strong heart, so I could tell our husband to go to hell!

LIZA. Ssh! Why would you tell him that?
SIKIRA. Not everytime but sometimes.
LIZA. That's silly – it isn't right for a wife to tell her husband to go to hell, without a reason.
SIKIRA. But what if he ...
LIZA. You must have a good reason for doing so; otherwise it's ... sheer rudeness – turn around.
SIKIRA. But he, too, acts rudeness-like to me sometimes.
LIZA. Raise your arm up.
SIKIRA. Then I feel like even running home to my mother.
LIZA. That's silly too. A woman doesn't run home to her mother everytime her husband treats her ... er ... "rudeness-like".
SIKIRA. Oohh, but you're leaving him.
LIZA. Sikira, my case is different. Or rather ... I think it is. He ...

[*She would say more, but checks herself.*]

SIKIRA. If you can leave him, *I* can leave him too.
LIZA [*trying hard to be calm about it*]. Sikira, he *lied* to me. At least, you knew he had two other women before you married him. But me ... he didn't tell me anything. When I walked into this house three weeks ago, I took you for a housemaid, and thought Mama Rashida was a washer-woman or something.
SIKIRA [*tickled*]. O ma se o!*
LIZA [*losing control*]. Well, it all goes to prove that Mr Rahman Lejoka-Brown does not have any respect whatsoever for my feelings. Why, I believe a woman must try to be a loving, loyal wife and all that. On the other hand, the husband must try to show some respect for the wife. After all, when we boil it down, men and women are all created equal, and unless a husband is ready to understand ...
SIKIRA. I like that!
LIZA. Like what?
SIKIRA. Men and women are created equal!
LIZA. Of course, we are all created equal. Why, there's nothing so strange about that fact – even though most men fail to accept it. Bend down let's see ...
SIKIRA [*filled with ideas*]. Sisi Liza! Suppose ... suppose ... suppose ...

[*Pauses; reconsiders her notion.*]

LIZA. Suppose what?

SIKIRA. Suppose we form a Party?
LIZA. Form a Party?
SIKIRA. Yes, for politics! All women in Nigeria. And then ...
LIZA [*amused*]. All women!
SIKIRA. All right ... Married women ...
  [*Crosses to one of* LEJOKA-BROWN's *posters.*]
Then we become Prime Ministers and campaign for election.
  [SIKIRA *yanks a poster off the wall, holds this high above her head like a banner, and starts marching round the living-room.*]
Then we sing ...
    Freedom, freedom,
    Everywhere there must be freedom.
LEJOKA-BROWN [*offstage*]. That's what they did in 1965.
  [LEJOKA-BROWN *and* OKONKWO *appear.*]
Same story. The bookheads came to me, begged me to help them form a Party.
  [*Stops short to cast an enquiring glance about, straining, as it were, to "sniff" the source of that Freedom chanting.*]
SIKIRA.
    Freedom for housewives,
    Freedom for all women.
    Yes, everywhere there must be freedom –
LEJOKA-BROWN [*poker-faced to* OKONKWO]. Someone has gone crazy?
OKONKWO. Looks like one of your wives must be feeling happy.
SIKIRA. Every home there must be freedom.
  [LEJOKA-BROWN *starts tip-toeing towards the house.* SIKIRA *is still prancing about in her spicily skimpy dress.* LIZA *is half slumped over her sewing-machine, convulsed with laughter at this unabashed caricaturing of* LEJOKA-BROWN *and his political antics.*]
SIKIRA.
    Freedom for mothers,
    Freedom for housemaids,
    Yes in every home there must be Freedom.
  [LEJOKA-BROWN *furtively pulls himself into the living-room, and stands within, larger than life!* SIKIRA *sees him, freezes, mouth agape, unnerved. Within seconds,* LIZA *notices him; she gulps down the rest of her laughter.*]
LEJOKA-BROWN [*dully to* SIKIRA]. Your legs: those of a baby antelope ... zig-zag in movement. What's the matter?
LIZA. Why, she's happy.

LEJOKA-BROWN. Is that so?

[*Still addressing* SIKIRA; *sarcastically.*]

Well, how much have you just won at the lottery, Sister? Where's the prize-money? Throw it down let's count.

LIZA. Must happiness depend on money alone? She is happy to be alive and free. Think of the boundless ecstasies of human freedom!

LEJOKA-BROWN [*to* LIZA, *with malevolent casualness*]. Are you there ... I am very happy too Woman. Very happy indeed, to notice that you have become used to this "gas chamber" house so much, that you have now begun a Communist-manifesto class in it.

LIZA. I see nothing wrong, not to say communistic, about the acquisition of some knowledge in the basics of freedom, Mr Lejoka-Brown.

LEJOKA-BROWN [*contemptuous*]. What basics? What d'you know about politics? I mean, hard-bone politics ... what basics?

LIZA [*doggedly*]. Why, fundamental human rights – irrespective of race, sex or creed. Oh, no. Nothing wrong, at all, Mr Lejoka-Brown! Particularly, where the "students" involved in the acquisition of such knowledge happen to be the wives of a freedom fighting hero on the national scene.

LEJOKA-BROWN [*hisses*]. Talking grammar!

[*Turns away, deciding it would be wiser not to get tangled up in an argument with this "Book-head"! He now directs his full attention at* SIKIRA *in her new, provocative dress!*]

LEJOKA-BROWN. What is that partly-hatched lizard dress for?

LIZA. Partly-hatched lizard!

SIKIRA. It is my dress for the Election Victory Celebrations.

LEJOKA-BROWN. I see.

[*Goes round her, pointing to the bare regions: the arms, shoulders, back, bosom.*]

What about this ... and here ... all these ... windows ... doors ... openings wider than two football fields put together! What photographer are you leaving them naked for?

SIKIRA [*running to a chair, picking up her dark veil*]. Sisi Liza will sew a veil for me ...

[*drapes veil over head.*]

... to cover the parts of my body you don't want open.

LEJOKA-BROWN [*with cynical calm contemplates the dress further then*]. Go take the rag off.

SIKIRA. Don't you like it?

LEJOKA-BROWN. Are you there.
 [*In a feigned voice of brotherly understanding.*]
Hurry along now and put on the type of dress human beings wear.

SIKIRA. But this is the type of dress they wear in America, and in England, and in ...

LEJOKA-BROWN. The devil take you and your America.

SIKIRA [*whining*]. B-u-t I l-i-k-e i-t!

LEJOKA-BROWN [*meanly whining in imitation*]. w-e-l-l I d-o-n-'t l-i-k-e i-t! Now, Woman, you do just as I say quick, or I'll tear off that half-peeled banana from the rest of your body!

SIKIRA. Do as *you* say, do as *you* say! It is always do as *you* say. Always command, command, command! Why don't you show some respect and let *me* do as *I* want, just once!
 [LEJOKA-BROWN *is bewildered by this sudden, unwonted boldness. He scowls accusingly at* LIZA, *then turns again to* SIKIRA.]

LEJOKA-BROWN. For the last time, Sister, let your feet take you into your room before thunder rumbles down your throat!

SIKIRA [*tearfully*]. What am I in this house, anyway?

LEJOKA-BROWN. Go on!

SIKIRA. Am I a slave?

LEJOKA-BROWN. You heard me!

SIKIRA. Or a housewife?

LEJOKA-BROWN [*berserk*]. You are one of the crazy headaches I've been crazy enough to get into my crazy head! Now get out of here!

SIKIRA [*to* LIZA]. You heard that?
 [*To* LEJOKA-BROWN, *backing away.*]
All right, all right, I will! I will get out of here.
 [*Rushes toward the rear door, stops, pokes her head round, and coos.*]
Men and women are created equal!
 [*Bolts out, slamming door shut quickly behind her.*]
 [LEJOKA-BROWN *casts a searching glance round the room, as if unsure of the source or owner of that defiant voice. He locates* LIZA, *and focuses his stare on her.*]

LEJOKA-BROWN. What was that you said, Sister?

OKONKWO. It wasn't Liza who spoke, Major.

LEJOKA-BROWN. Woman, I ask you: What's this school-girl arithmetic talk about one Man equals one Woman?

[*No answer. He advances hostilely toward* LIZA.]

All right, Lady Sophistication ...

LIZA. I dare you to touch me!

LEJOKA-BROWN [*removing his voluminous robe, leaving only the singlet and pantaloons on*]. The time has come when I, too, must give some lessons of my own.

[LIZA *begins to leave.* LEJOKA-BROWN *steps forward, seizes her by the arm, and jerks her back.*]

OKONKWO. Major, please ...

LEJOKA-BROWN. You keep out of this!

[OKONKWO *leaves.*]

Wife, it is too much indulgence that makes the she-goat grow a long beard like her husband, the he-goat. You hear? Now, I'm no longer going to lie down forever like an over-fed boa constrictor, while you wipe foot on all the moral standards I have set in this house!

LIZA. Have I interfered in any ...

LEJOKA-BROWN. Interfered! Ha! *La ku li ju lai lu!** My dear woman, *you* have sunk to the low, low, low *bottom* of moral mud!

LIZA. Moral mud!

LEJOKA-BROWN. Beyond compare, Sister. You're not the Liza I married in the Congo! But, Allah being my Helper, as your husband still, even though you refuse to accept that now, nevertheless, it is my duty to lead you back to the path of righteousness!

LIZA. Mr Lejoka-Brown, I could sue you for defamation of character!

LEJOKA-BROWN. First and foremost! You must see to it that all areas around, above, and below your shoulders are well covered up from now on. No more short knickers, and no more ...

[*Indicates the tight Capri pants* LIZA *is wearing.*]

... tight, tight, tight trousers that show all your ... your ... Geography! Furthermore ...

[*Grabs her packet of cigarettes, and crushes it in his fist.*]

Cigarette smoking will have to stop – now! And last of all,

starting from this night, I want to see you act as *my* wife. That's all!

[*Turns to go into rear of house.*]

LIZA. And where does your "moral mud" bit com ₁?

LEJOKA-BROWN. Why, I have just named them all.

LIZA [*in a fit*]. Oooohhhh ...

[*Picks up a broom from the floor.*]

You ...

[*She swings broom wildly in the direction of* LEJOKA-BROWN *who ducks,* LIZA *misses, and the force of that attack sends her careening across the living-room.* LEJOKA-BROWN *lunges forward, catches her.*]

LEJOKA-BROWN. Attention!

[*Steadies her.*]

Now ready, aim, fire!

[*Spanks her on the buttocks, and hops back.*]

[*Maddened by this teasing,* LIZA *again lurches more desperately after* LEJOKA-BROWN, *striking blindly with the broom. One wallop gets* LEJOKA-BROWN *full on the thigh, forcing him to retreat through the rear door into the backyard, hotly pursued by* LIZA. *At this point we see* MAMA RASHIDA *approaching. On her head is the basket cage housing some live chickens. Simultaneously,* SIKIRA *rushes in from rear of house. On her head is a large trunk box. She hastens across the living-room, kicks door open, and bolts out, almost bumping into* MAMA RASHIDA.]

MAMA RASHIDA. A-ah! What's happening? Sikira!

SIKIRA. I'm going home to my mother!

MAMA RASHIDA [*trotting after her, chickens squawking*]. Wait! Answer me ... what's the matter?

SIKIRA [*leaving*]. **Our husband has gone mad again!**

[LEJOKA-BROWN *and* LIZA *"fight" back into the living-room.* LIZA *is still wielding a broom.* LEJOKA-BROWN, *now in singlet and underpants, deftly parries* LIZA'S *blows with the lid of a trash can which he handles like a shield. They fight on – the one attacking, the other defending: both panting and puffing.* MAMA RASHIDA *hurries back from pursuing* SIKIRA.]

MAMA RASHIDA. My lord, my lord. Sikira is gone!

[LEJOKA-BROWN *drops his guard and turns to* MAMA RASHIDA. LIZA *seizes this chance, whacks a final blow, catching* LEJOKA-BROWN *full on the rump.*]

LEJOKA-BROWN [*turning slowly to* LIZA, *absorbing the pain*]. Foul play, Elizabeth!

BLACKOUT

SCENE IV

POLYCARP *is sitting at the main entrance, guarding it. A Caucasian* BBC CORRESPONDENT *is on the porch awaiting admittance.*

BBC CORRESPONDENT. When did the executive meeting start?
POLYCARP. I no know, Oga.
BBC CORRESPONDENT. Very well then, when will it be over?
POLYCARP. I no know, Oga.
BBC CORRESPONDENT. Listen, friend, the Major invited me here ...
 [*Digs out his identity card and shows* POLYCARP.]
... this evening – six o'clock. I'm a BBC correspondent.
POLYCARP. Maybe dat be true, Mister. But na dat same Major wey say make I no let any person enter tele-e he tell me so.
BBC CORRESPONDENT. So tell him I'm here –
POLYCARP. I always do whetin di Major tell me, Mister. If Major say jump, I jump! 'e say stand, I tanda; butu, I butu; 'e say run – na four-forty dat!
 [*Two local press* REPORTERS *and a* PHOTOGRAPHER *approach house.*]
LOCAL REPORTER 1. I understand he has three wives.
LOCAL REPORTER 2. Now two. The youngest left him last week, two remaining – one of whom is a qualified medic, graduated from America.
LOCAL REPORTER 1. Really!
LOCAL REPORTER 2. Pretty as a young palmtree!
 [*They meet the* BBC CORRESPONDENT *on the porch.*]
BBC CORRESPONDENT. How d'you do?
LOCAL REPORTER 1 [*shaking hands introducing himself*]. Mallam Rothman Zamberiberi, Daily Brigade.
BBC CORRESPONDENT. Phillip MacDonald – BBC.
LOCAL REPORTER 2. Etim Bassey – Sunday Spectator.

LOCAL REPORTER 1. Can we go in?
BBC CORRESPONDENT. This gentleman here says no.
LOCAL REPORTER 2. No?
LOCAL REPORTERS AND PHOTOGRAPHER [*together*] Why, it's past six already.
Kilo de, Oga?
Mister, whas matter wey you no 'gree we enter?
POLYCARP. One by each, Mister Gentlemen, talk one by each!
[LEJOKA-BROWN *enters living-room from backyard in company of* OSAGIE *and* GASKIYA.]
LEJOKA-BROWN. P-o-l-y-c-a-r-p!
POLYCARP [*rushing in*]. Beg to report, sah! Four men dey wahala me outside, sah. Dhem say dhem wan' see ...
LEJOKA-BROWN. Oh, are you there – please – come right in gentlemen.
[*Ushers the newsmen in, poses for a couple of camera snaps.*]
Sorry to have kept you waiting. We were just rounding up some urgent executive matters. How d'you do? Make yourselves at home, gentlemen.
[*Men settle in chairs, taking out their notebooks and pencils. Meanwhile,* LEJOKA-BROWN *is having a tete-a-tete with* POLYCARP, *away from the gathering.*]
Where is Liza?
POLYCARP. She go Bar Beach, Major.
LEJOKA-BROWN [*alarmed*]. Bar bea ...! Look here, when she comes back, don't let her come in through here, you hear.
POLYCARP. I hear sah!
LEJOKA-BROWN. Now hurry bring drinks, bring drinks.
[*Turns to newsmen.*]
Well, well, well. Now, Honourable Gentlemen of the World Press. We have invited you here this evening, to *see* for yourselves. There are rumours and rumours and rumours that the Deputy Leader of my Party, Mallam Gaskiya ...
[*Takes* MALLAM GASKIYA *by the arm.*]
and I are hammering one another in a hot, hot, struggle for power.
[*He hoists up* MALLAM GASKIYA'S *arm in a jaunty gesture of amity.*]
Now, Gentlemen, *see* for yourselves!
[*Camera-flash catches* LEJOKA-BROWN *and* MALLAM GASKIYA. LEJOKA-BROWN *grins genially in appreciation of the photographer's timing, then continues.*]

The breeze in our nation smells with rotten stories that the Secretary-General of my Party, Mr Osagie ...

[*Clasps* OSAGIE'S *arm.*]

... and I, do not see eye to eye any more. But Gentlemen ...

[*Raises* OSAGIE'S *arm and strikes a gay pose.*]

See for yourselves!

[*Again the obliging photographer responds.* LEJOKA-BROWN *sits down with dramatic finality.*]

Questions!

NEWSMEN [*together*]. Mr Lejoka-Brown ...
                   Mr Lejoka-Brown ...
                   Mr President ...
                   Sir ...

LEJOKA-BROWN. Turn by turn, Gentlemen, turn by turn, o! Daily Herald man, you talk.

LOCAL REPORTER I. Mr Lejoka-Brown, with only five months before elections, and in the light of widespread rumours of a rift within your Party, what are your chances of victory at the forthcoming elections?

LEJOKA-BROWN. Thank you!

[*Springs to his feet again.*]

Well, Gentlemen of the Press, you have come, and you have seen for yourselves. Not only are all members of my Party at peace with one another, we have never ...

[*His voice rising with rhetorical fervour.*]

I repeat, never: never before have all members of my Party been more united, and never have we felt more confident of victory at the polls than now!

[*Applause by all – started by* MR OSAGIE, *supported by* MALLAM GASKIYA *and courteously reinforced by members of the Press. Silence again.* LEJOKA-BROWN *looks over the shoulder of a reporter, flippantly dictating what he thinks the spelling of polls is.*]

Polls – p-o-l-e-s.

REPORTER. Beg your pardon.

LEJOKA-BROWN. I said p-o-l-e-s: polls.

BBC CORRESPONDENT. It's P-o-l-l-s, Mr President.

LEJOKA-BROWN. I see ... anyhow, polls is poles. Next question. BBC man, your turn.

[POLYCARP *has finished serving drinks: he now goes to the porch to watch out for* LIZA'S *arrival.*]

BBC CORRESPONDENT. Would any of you, Sirs . . .
  [*Indicates* MR OSAGIE *and* MALLAM GASKIYA.]
. . . care to make a statement in regard to Mr Lejoka-Brown's assertion that all is well with your party?
MALLAM GASKIYA. No, no – Mr Lejoka-Brown's statement is final.
LEJOKA-BROWN. Wonderful!
OSAGIE. He speaks for us all.
LEJOKA-BROWN. Fantastic! Well, Gentlemen!
  [*Extends an arm to shake hands with a local reporter.*]
The truth is in your hands. In your hands, too, my dear Editor of the Sunday Spectator.
  [*Turns to another.*]
And in your hands, my dear correspondent of the British Broadcasting Corporation! That is all we have to say, Gentlemen. The rest is in your hands . . . the truth is in your hands . . . the ball of facts is at your feet! Now, go out and *kick* it!
  [*Applause; he turns to reach for his drink.*]
But, before you go from here, Gentlemen, do join us in a hearty sip . . .
  [*Raises glass.*]
. . . to the health and success of the . . .
  [*Car hums to a stop offstage.*]
POLYCARP [*calling from outside*]. Major!
  [*Guests begin to reach for their glasses.* POLYCARP *bursts in, stands agitatedly within door.*]
LEJOKA-BROWN. One and only National Libera . . .
POLYCARP [*urgently*]. Major!
LEJOKA-BROWN [*putting glass down*]. Excuse me, Gentlemen . . .
  [*Goes to* POLYCARP *who whispers something in his ear.* LEJOKA-BROWN *pulls back from* POLYCARP, *turns to stare at the Guests. They stare back blankly, baffled.* LEJOKA-BROWN *hurries to the porch, looks out and barks at someone a distance away.*]
Go back! Don't come in like that . . . you hear? Go back I . . .
  [*Swoops suddenly back into living-room, draws blind quickly over window, spins around to confront the guests who are now pressing close on him, curious.*]
Back, all of you! Bloody busy-bodies! Get back I . . .
  [*Shoves them roughly away from the vicinity of the window.*]
Kitchen! Into the kitchen, everybody! I say go into . . .
  [*Group gapes at him, lost.*]

Oohoo! You won't, hunh? All right ...

[*He lunges toward wall, whips out matchet from sheath, dives toward kitchen door, flings it open.*]

Come on, everybody!

[*Changes his mind, slams door shut.*]

All right ... All right – on the floor! Every blinking man, on the blinking floor I say!

[*Guests begin to sink to kneeling position on the floor.*]

Whiteman!

[*To* BBC CORRESPONDENT *who has been trying to peep through window.*]

You know Kiriji war? Oooh! Go read your history on Yoruba wars. With this matchet ... are you there ... with this ... *agedengbe**, my grandfather chopped off fifty-three human heads in Kiriji War! Now, you do as I say or ...

[*Flies at him.* BBC CORRESPONDENT *scuttles away from window and cowers in a kneeling position with the others. Meanwhile,* LEJOKA-BROWN *has decided against the efficacy of a matchet. He yanks rifle from wall.*]

All right! Face down everybody! Flat! Like lizards!

[*Guests sink down, prone on the bare floor.* LEJOKA-BROWN *trains his rifle at them.*]

I dare anyone of you to look up before I tell you to. By God and Allah, if I don't blast off your groins as I did to those long-nosed Belgians in the Congo, call me a bastard!

[LIZA *steps into full view. She is scantily clad in a bathing suit – a bikini. She walks gingerly onto porch, opens front door, enters, sees the assembly of decently dressed gentlemen humbled in idiotic prostration on the bare floor. She halts, taken aback.*]

LIZA. Hey!
LEJOKA-BROWN. To your room!
LIZA. What is this?
LEJOKA-BROWN. You heard me!
LIZA. A military exercise?
LEJOKA-BROWN. I said go to your room, o!
LIZA. Now wait a minute.
LEJOKA-BROWN. Go! You cheap, street woman!

[*Shocked, a hand clasped over her mouth in horror. Someone in the prostrate group whistles.*]

LEJOKA-BROWN. Who did that?

[*Aims his rifle searchingly at group.*]

LIZA. Me? A cheap street woman?

LEJOKA-BROWN [*still addressing group*]. Are you there? I said who whistled that crazy, night-club whistle?

[*Nobody stirs.*]

You fear to talk, hunh? I see ... but you're not afraid to whistle like a crazy sailor inside this sacred house of my fathers!

LIZA. All right, fellow, this time you've had it!

[*She storms into rear of house, slamming door fitfully behind her. With* LIZA *out of the way,* LEJOKA-BROWN *goes to put the rifle away, takes a deep breath, relieved.*]

LEJOKA-BROWN. Well, gentlemen! Danger over! Up now, everybody – as you were! Stand up ... "stand up, stand up for Jesus ..." as the Christians sing ...

[*One by one, men begin to pick themselves sullenly up.* LEJOKA-BROWN *calmly reaches for his drink, raises the glass in toast, facing the squad of dust-encrusted, glum-faced guests, and intones expansively.*]

Gentlemen! C-h-e-e-rs.

BLACKOUT

SCENE V

Same day. Conference room. Applause and excitement as members re-assemble for the climax of the National Liberation Party's meeting. Besides members of the Liberation Party, we see a delegation of women, prominent among whom is SIKIRA. *Sitting beside* SIKIRA, *is* MADAM AJANAKU, *the President of the National Union of Nigerian Market Women. She is, of course,* SIKIRA's *mother.* LEJOKA-BROWN *is notably absent.*

MALLAM GASKIYA. Be seated, Ladies and Gentlemen!

A MEMBER. Silence!

MALLAM GASKIYA. The Emergency Committee of the National Liberation Party will now resume its deliberations.

[*Gestures to* OSAGIE.]

OSAGIE. Ladies and Gentlemen, Mr Lejoka-Brown's disgraceful behaviour at the news conference this evening has further demonstrated his outright contempt for, and gross callousness toward the feelings and dignity of members of our beloved Party!

[*Applause.*]

Even the honourable delegates of the Market Women's Union are beginning to lose faith in the stability, and intent of the National Liberation Party. Oohh no. Ladies and Gentlemen, we cannot ...

[*Becomes fiery.*]

We can no longer afford to risk the future of this Party. We can no longer afford to compromise the noble ideals of the National Liberation Party, with the abjectly myopic, not to say, old-fashioned, authoritarian leadership of Mr Rahman Lejoka-Brown. My beloved brothers and sisters, I appeal to you! In the proverbial wisdom of our forebears – when the vine entwines your roof ... it is time to cut it!

[*Sits. General talking pervades the room.*]

MALLAM GASKIYA [*striking a gavel for silence*]. The house will now give the floor to the Honourable President of the National Market Women's Union. Ladies and Gentlemen – Madam Bambina Uchenna Ajanaku.

[MADAM AJANAKU *rises – a physically grand mountain of a woman. Applause. Gavel strikes. Silence.*]

MADAM AJANAKU. Ehn ... Agbanikaka man say: die cow wey no get tail for nyash, na God nahim de helep am drive fly commot. No more no less. Ehn ... me I no sabi grammar o; me and book no be one-mama-one-papa. But God helep me, I know how di worl' dey turn and me too I sabi turn am, gaan. So when I talk, I know wetin I dey talk.

[*Calm and mordant.*]

Ehn ... Since whey* una oga marry dis my pickin ...

[*Pushes* SIKIRA *forward.*]

... one year don pass. No more no less. Dat no bad. Me nko? I be tru-born Owerri woman. But I marry Yoruba ... Ehn no be di promote whey I wan' promote national unity nahim me too I go carry my pickin go give Lejoka-Brown for marry? I no know say na mango-mango,* manafiki* man nahim Lejoka-Brown be, o! No more, no less.

[*Clears her throat.*]

So now, last week ago, dis una* Lejoka-Brown, abi na Lejoka-Yellow he say him be sef, he come kick my pickin commot for house throway for outside like dog. Na so ... na so una oga take suffer suffer my pickin wey I give am for 'yawo. No more no less, o. Now ... Una ask me whetin I think about una Party? Una wan' to know how my Union feel about una Party? All right, I go tell una whetin I think about una Party. I go let you know how my Union peepul dem feel about una Party. So make una put yess* for ground! Una Party be like person mouth!

ONE MEMBER [*a rotund, portly fellow*]. Like what?

MADAM AJANAKU [*irritated by the interruption*]. I say, una Party be like person mouth, big-belle man. What's matter? You deaf? Una Party dey hungry for we women vote? Ehn we go give una plenty vote to full una belle double, BUT ... broder me, una no go fit eat di vote, o. Because why? Because una mout' get one bad teet' inside inside. And una mout' go get wahala* tel-e-e-e una take dhat rotten teet' commot!
[*Thumps her chest heavily.*]
Na me Bambina, talk so! No more no less.
[*Tense silence.*]

A MEMBER. Mr Chairman ... I ... move that a vote of no confidence be cast on the leadership of Mr Raham Lejoka-Brown.

ANOTHER MEMBER. Motion seconded.

A WOMAN [*apparently an educated, hired secretary*]. Point of correction. We members of the National Market Women's Union would rather move that Mr Lejoka-Brown be voted out of office completely.

WOMEN. Hear, hear!
Na so! Na so!
Na dhat we want!

WOMAN. Another candidate must be nominated by this House to contest elections in place of Mr Lejoka-Brown, in his constituency.
[*Women cheer.*]

MADAM AJANAKU. And dis time na woman candidate nahim we want, o! Woman candidate. No more no less.

MALLAM GASKIYA. Ladies and Gentlemen, I suggest we adjourn for ten minutes so that members of the Party Executive can hold consultations in view of present developments.

MADAM AJANAKU. Dat na too much grammar. We want woman candidate – una 'gree abi una no 'gree. We no dey beg una. Political Party dem bocoo* for country; dem dey wait for we vote.

MALLAM GASKIYA [*leading executive members out*]. We shall be back in about fifteen minutes.

MADAM AJANAKU. Na una sabi!

[*Leads her group out.*]

When una talk munumunumunu finish make una fin' me come for my house. Abi?

[*To audience.*]

Man wey carry Ogbono* soup-pot for hand, and di man wey carry foo-foo* for head, na who go fin' who go?

[*Shrugs.*]

No more no less?

[*Leads women off.*]

FADE OUT

SCENE VI

LEJOKA-BROWN'S *living-room. Polycarp enters carrying an ironing board. He sets this down near the settee and exits, as Liza appears hugging an armful of dresses for pressing. Soon after,* LEJOKA-BROWN *himself walks in, stands within the door-frame, contemplating* LIZA. *In his hand is a book – the Holy Koran.*

LEJOKA-BROWN. What's this I hear about your leaving the country?

[LIZA *disregards him; goes about her business.*]

I refused to go to an emergency Party meeting because I wanted to . . . to talk to you Elizabeth.

[*Moves towards her.*]

Can we now sit down and talk . . . like two human beings?

LIZA. Sorry, I've got no time for . . .

LEJOKA-BROWN [*putting a hand gently on her shoulder*]. This is how you've been acting ever since you came here – stubbornly avoiding me.

LIZA. Mr Lejoka-Brown, please get . . .

[*She moves away from him.*]

LEJOKA-BROWN. Always behaving like a pond that stands proudly aloof from a river, as though water weren't common to both of them. My Koran says only Allah has the right to judge and condemn, Elizabeth. I don't know what your Bible says. But as human beings, I am begging you to forgive all that has . . .

LIZA. Forgive! Ha! After that . . . Oh, what's the use? It serves me right, anyhow. I should have got out of here long ago and sued for immediate divorce. But like the idiotic daydreamer that I am, I kept hoping that after the elections, you'd come back to being the man I once knew in the Congo, and we'd sort things out honourably. But what is my reward? You called me "a cheap, street woman", right in the presence of . . .

LEJOKA-BROWN. Face downwards Liza! I had everybody facing down like lizards so they wouldn't know whom I was angry at! Besides, if not that you, too, simply wanted to get me angry, don't you know that my religion is against women opening their bodies to public eyes? You never used to dress like that – now suddenly . . .

LIZA. That is no reason to call me – oh, what's the use!
[*Concentrates on her chore.*]

LEJOKA-BROWN. The cause of all this is my marriages, I admit. But if you will only let me explain the background –

LIZA. Go right ahead. Who's stopping you? Say all you want!

LEJOKA-BROWN. Mama Rashida for instance. After my elder brother died, my father married her to me according to the will of Allah which is contained in these words of the Holy Prophet Muhammed, *sallallahu alayhi wa sallam**:
[*Opens Koran and reads from it.*]
Al sai alal armalati wal miskin kal mujahid ti sabil Allahi.
"He who helps the widow or a poor person is like one who walks in the path of Allah!"

MAMA RASHIDA [*calling from offstage*]. Sister Liza!

LEJOKA-BROWN. Now, Elizabeth, who am I to oppose the will of Allah? I'd planned to help Mama Rashida as much as I could without letting you find out because I was afraid you might not understand. And as for Sikira, I only wanted her to help me win the elections, Liza. Believe me. If I could become a Minister, someone you would feel proud to call your husband, I would then have . . .

LIZA. Mr Lejoka-Brown, your material possessions or status in life mean nothing to me where my love is concerned, understand?

LEJOKA-BROWN. All women say that!

LIZA [*hurt*]. Is that so! Very well then, if you think you can make me happy only after you've become the Prime Minister of the whole Continent of Africa and be riding in a hundred Rolls Royces strung together, with money strewn on the ground for me to walk on, then you are no more the Rahman Lejoka-Brown I once loved – no!

MAMA RASHIDA [*hurries in excitedly, carrying a basket full of eggs*]. Sister come see . . .

[*Stops short, sensing trouble.*]

LIZA. You've now become a depraved, no-good scoundrel with the tastes of a pig, obsessed with the putrescent values of a maggot! Now . . .

[*Roughly gathers her clothes together.*]

. . . get out of my life!

[*Bulldozes her way past him.*]

LEJOKA-BROWN. Elizabeth, please . . .

[*Lurches after Liza, bumps a foot against a chair, missing her. Hops back to settee, absorbing the pain.*]

MAMA RASHIDA. What's the matter, my lord?

LEJOKA-BROWN. With my toes?

MAMA RASHIDA. No, with Liza.

LEJOKA-BROWN. Oh. She says she's going home.

MAMA RASHIDA. Hunh? And what is my lord doing to stop her?

LEJOKA-BROWN. Bumping my toes against a chair!

MAMA RASHIDA. Is that so? Very well then, perhaps you'd better start bumping into another woman who will take care of the house after Liza leaves, because if you think I will leave my big new trade and stay home all day, you mistake!

[*She exits in a huff,* LEJOKA-BROWN *gaping after her with horrified disbelief.*]

OKONKWO [*hurrying in*]. Major! . . . Is the Major in?

[*Swings door open and enters breathlessly.*]

Major . . . your Party has just . . .

LEJOKA-BROWN. Forget politics brother!

OKONKWO. What's the matter?

LEJOKA-BROWN. Women are taking over the world!

OKONKWO. What d'you mean?
LEJOKA-BROWN. We have come to a new world, brother. A woman's world!
[*Warningly.*]
Are you sure you still want to get married?
OKONKWO. What are you talking about?
LEJOKA-BROWN. I tried to talk to Liza; Liza ran out swearing she'd leave me forever! Seconds later, good old Mama Rashida danced in here, handed me an ultimatum, and walked out!
OKONKWO. Mama Rashida! Leaving too?
LEJOKA-BROWN [*nodding weightily*]. A woman's world, I tell you!
OKONKWO. Water don pass garri* tru-tru! Where is Liza now?
LEJOKA-BROWN. In her woman's room, packing her woman's things.
[OKONKWO *makes for the rear rooms.*]
LEJOKA-BROWN [*bawling out*]. Mama Rashida!
[*No answer.*]
Mama Rash . . .
MAMA RASHIDA [*appearing*]. Here I am, my lord.
[LEJOKA-BROWN *gestures her to come closer. She does.* LEJOKA-BROWN *sits down, passes his hands prayerfully over his face.*]
LEJOKA-BROWN. Un surni Ya – Allah! Mama Rashida, first wife of my older brother: may Allah rest his soul in perfect peace! For four years since we've been living together, haven't I been treating you well and with respect? I gave you money to trade . . .
MAMA RASHIDA. True, my lord, and for all that, may Allah the All-Providing *supply* you profit.
LEJOKA-BROWN [*exaggeratedly*]. *Amin, Ya Rabbi! Barakallah lana wa lakum!** Now, why are you behaving to me like an unbeliever?
MAMA RASHIDA. I'm not running away, my lord, if that is what you think.
LEJOKA-BROWN. No?
[*Raises hands Heavenwards in gratitude.*]
Alhamdu Lillāh*!
MAMA RASHIDA. Alhaji Mustafa –
LEJOKA-BROWN. You want to marry him!
MAMA RASHIDA. Oh no, my lord!

LEJOKA-BROWN [*sighs with relief*]. *Arhamni Ya – Allah!**
MAMA RASHIDA. Alhaji Mustafa says my chickens will grow better in the village where there is much land, and life is peaceful.
LEJOKA-BROWN. Ehe-en?
MAMA RASHIDA. So, if my lord will talk to Alhaji Mustafa . . .
[*Tries to impress him with her new learning.*]
. . . who has plenty land to *supply*; and if my lord will ask him for *Demand*, he will sell it to us for *Capital*. Now, I can then go to the village farm and start my big new trade there. My lord can come to see old Mama Rashida and her chicken farm in Abule Oja whenever he wants. But . . . my lord must make sure he brings Sisi Liza along whenever he comes to visit because I shall need her help in working my chicken trade.
LEJOKA-BROWN. I see.
MAMA RASHIDA. Well . . . what does my lord think?
[*No answer.*]
I . . . I could take Polycarp along with me to the farm. I'll be safe.
LEJOKA-BROWN. You really want it that way?
MAMA RASHIDA. But my lord, how else could I make plenty *capital* to *supply* you for politics, if you *demand* on *interest* at *ten per cent* for over . . .
LEJOKA-BROWN. All right, all right . . .
[*Enter Okonkwo from rear rooms.*]
OKONKWO. Major.
LEJOKA-BROWN [*To* MAMA RASHIDA]. Go tell Alhaji Mustafa I want to see him.
MAMA RASHIDA [*ecstatically*]. I thank you, my lord. May Allah grant you more . . .
LEJOKA-BROWN [*easing her off*]. Ami, ami, ami* – tell the driver to take you to the Alhaji, and bring him here.
[MAMA RASHIDA *exits.*]
OKONKWO. Major, Liza is coming to see you.
LEJOKA-BROWN. See me?
OKONKWO. She . . . I . . . I gave her a message for you.
LEJOKA-BROWN. What message?
OKONKWO [*leaving*]. She'll tell you. I'll be back later.
[*Exits, as we hear a knocking on the rear door.* LEJOKA-BROWN *primps himself. Another knock.*]

LEJOKA-BROWN. Who is it?
LIZA. Me.
  [LIZA *enters and crosses over to sit on settee.* LEJOKA-BROWN *stares at her, wondering. Some moments of awkward silence. Finally,* LEJOKA-BROWN *ventures a line.*]
LEJOKA-BROWN. You ... you have come to ... say good-bye?
  [*No answer.*]
  Well ... what is it?
LIZA [*haltingly*]. Mr Okonkwo has just told me that ... you have been ... voted out of office by your Party.
  [LEJOKA-BROWN *absorbs the news calmly. Then with a sigh.*]
LEJOKA-BROWN. I see ... I thank you.
LIZA. What are you going to do now?
LEJOKA-BROWN. Fight.
  [*Crosses to get the rifle.*]
LIZA. Fight! Fight whom?
LEJOKA-BROWN [*blowing dust off rifle*]. That's for me to know, and an outsider to find out.
LIZA. Outsider! Who? Me?
LEJOKA-BROWN. What does it matter to you now, whom I fight? I am now alone, and I think and act alone.
LIZA. Don't you think I have a right to know? Don't you think I care?
LEJOKA-BROWN. Oh, come now, Liza, this no time to weep! Now is time for action. Are you with me or not?
  [*No answer.*]
  I said are you ...
LIZA. What d'you want me to do?
LEJOKA-BROWN [*with exaggerated glee*]. Ahaa! Now you talk like a good, loving wife who understands. Here ...
  [*Dumps rifle on her lap.*]
  ... take that!
LIZA. Why?
LEJOKA-BROWN. Don't you see? All my plans for politics are now: Chuuu! I can't be Minister anymore. So now this is my secret ...
  [*Throws an arm over* LIZA's *shoulders and pulls her close.*]
  You stand by with this rifle, and when the crazy Government comes along one fine morning to tear down this *shrine* of my forefathers ...
  [*Sings a war chant dancing in the process.*]

Gbogungboro,	Gbogungboro
l'o l'oke Anoye	Lord at Anoye hill
Odidi ọmọ afodidi gun	Odidi, Chief of pluggers!
Ofi wadi gun	He plugs the channel of invaders
O f'ehindi gun	He plugs the retreat of vandals
Odidi ọmọ afodidi gun	Odidi, Chief of pluggers!
Ayanmode, baba ogbẹ	Gaping ulcer – father of all wounds
Odidi ọmọ afodidi gun	Odidi – you skilled dealer of matchet blows!

[*Changes song.*]

Ogun Ọyọ kẹrẹkan	The fight with Oyo
Ogun Ọyọ masiku o	is yet to be re-fought
Imọrimọ jojo	The clash with Oyo
Ogun Ọyọ masiku o	is yet to be decisive: awesome confrontation – that, when it does come!

[*He yanks* LIZA *off her feet, and shoves her headlong in mock battle.*]
Shoulder to shoulder we'll fight like two hungry demons!

LIZA. Fight the Government?

LEJOKA-BROWN. Ssshhh! You're not deserting me so soon, are you?

LIZA. But how can we fight the...

LEJOKA-BROWN. Stand by me! You promised: "for better, for worse!"

LIZA. But what if we get killed?

LEJOKA-BROWN. Then "Death will do us part." Come on!
[*Jerks her closer.*]
First, you must learn the ten basic firing positions...
[*Forces her down to her knees.*]
A marksman is no marksman, unless he knows what to do...
[*She flops on her stomach.*]
The prone position...
[*Pulls her up to a sitting position.*]
the cross ankle position –

LIZA. We can't!

LEJOKA-BROWN. Says who?
[*Seizes her by the arm, races across the living room to duck behind settee.*]
The foxhole posi...

LIZA. Just the two of us? It's impossible, believe me!

LEJOKA-BROWN. Nonsense! Okonkwo and I fought seventy-seven long-nosed Belgians in the Congo for five and a half days, without food, without water . . .

[*Hurls her up and over the settee.*]

LIZA. But Okonkwo is a man, I'm a woman!

LEJOKA-BROWN. Sshhh! *Men and women are created equal*, remember!

The kneeling supported posi . . .

LIZA. No!

[*She collapses on the settee, exhausted, angry.*]

What kind of a man are you, anyway? Your whole world is falling apart, and all you think about is your past army life and your crazy politics! Ugh!

[*She gets ready to storm out again, but this time* LEJOKA-BROWN *catches her, wraps her in a tender embrace, kissing her forehead.*]

LEJOKA-BROWN. Are you there . . . Elizabeth, I'm really very sorry for everything that has happened. I'll go back to the cocoa business. No more monkey politics for me. But first I'll build you the clinic I promised. On this very land. I'll make sacrifice to my fathers, and then break down this old house. I'll build a new one on its soil. Three stories. You'll use two for the Clinic, and we'll live in peace on the top floor.

[*Angry with himself.*]

I was doing fine with the cocoa business, anyhow, before crazy politics came and turned my head upside down like . . .

OKONKWO [*approaching house*]. Major!

LIZA. Someone's calling. I think it's Mr Okonkwo.

LEJOKA-BROWN. Aaahhh . . . You sit down!

[*Sits her down on his lap.*]

OKONKWO. M-a-j-o-r!

LEJOKA-BROWN. Let him crow!

[LEJOKA-BROWN *starts kissing* LIZA *tenderly on the arm.*]

OKONKWO. Is the Major in?

[*Opens door and enters.*]

Maj . . .

[*He freezes, gawking at* LIZA *and* LEJOKA-BROWN. *With exaggerated smacking of the lips,* LEJOKA-BROWN *starts pecking at* LIZA's *ear-lobe.* OKONKWO *crosses himself, turns away, surprised, embarrassed.*]

LEJOKA-BROWN. Attention!
[OKONKWO *stiffens at attention.*]
Are you there? I could have you court-martialled for breaking my concentration on the Egg Treatment!

OKONKWO. Beg your pardon, Major.

LIZA. The Egg Treatment?
[*Chuckles.*]
What's that?

LEJOKA-BROWN. Emm... A military strategy.
[*To* OKONKWO.]
As you were!
[OKONKWO *relaxes.*]
So what's the crowing all about?

OKONKWO. Come take a look at your Party's new candidate for the elections, Major!

LEJOKA-BROWN. Aahh... I'm through with politics, brother.
[*Crowd appears in a procession singing the National Liberation Party's parade song.*]

CROWD. Freedom, freedom,
    Everywhere there must
    be freedom.
[*Borne shoulder-high in an open sedan is someone whose beaming face looks very familiar to us:* SIKIRA.]

SIKIRA. [*declaiming*]. Rise up! All women of our land! Rise up and vote for freedom, or forever be slaves!

LEJOKA-BROWN. Who is that crab?

OKONKWO [*looking out through the window*]. Come have a peep, Major.
[LEJOKA-BROWN *hesitates.*]

SIKIRA. Vote... vote for me! It is true I am a woman, but that does not matter. It does not matter, because why? Because...

LEJOKA-BROWN. A woman?
[LEJOKA-BROWN *and* LIZA, *curious, make for the front door in time to see and hear* SIKIRA *say.*]

SIKIRA. MEN AND WOMEN ARE CREATED EQUAL!

MADAM AJANAKU. No more, no less!
[*Crowd cheers uproariously, dancing and singing as the procession goes out. Slow fade on* LEJOKA-BROWN *who is consolingly embraced by a surprised and excited* LIZA.]

OKONKWO. Well, major, how now?
LEJOKA-BROWN. Are you there ...
  [*Gravely.*]
The world has come to an end!

FINALE

GLOSSARY

Page 4 *Wallahi:* an abbreviation of the Arabic expression "Wa Allah, Ta-Allah" that has become *"Wallahi Tallahi"* in the Yoruba vernacular. It means "God is my witness".

7 *Unsurni ya Allah:* An Arabic exclamation – "Help me, O Allah!"

8 *Jagajaga:* A Nigerian pidgin English word for chaos, disorderliness, confusion.

11 *L a rahbaniyya fil Islam:* A quote from the Holy Koran; its figurative sense here is: "Celibacy in Islam? Never!"

13 *Iyawo* or *'yawo:* Yoruba word for housewife.

14 *Arhamni Ya – Allah:* Arabic prayer: "show mercy on me, O Allah."

18 *Ase:* Yoruba word for Amen.

23 *K'abo:* Yoruba word meaning "welcome!"

'tory leke plasas: a Nigerian pidgin English expression with a gossipy smack. It means: "the story has the piquant appeal of vegetable stew (*plasas*)."

Ogongo: Yoruba word for ostrich. Sikira is implying, in metaphorical pidgin English, that the story of Lejoka-Brown's politics makes big news (*ie* a big bird worth talking about).

25 Bobby Benson's *Taxi Driver Highlife*: Bobby Benson is a popular Nigerian musician. This composition, based on a folk tune and played to Highlife beat, was among the musical hits in Nigeria about the mid-fifties.

Highlife: A social dance-music popular in West Africa – particularly in Ghana where it is believed to have originated, and Nigeria.

Tele: Pidgin for the adverb "till" or "until".

29 O. N: *is* Order of the Niger: a Nigerian title of Honour awarded in recognition of one's meritorious service to the Nation. Lejoka-Brown is assuming that he will automatically be so accoladed after leading his party to victory at the polls.

29 M.H.R.: a non-titular abbreviation for Member of the (Nigerian) House of Representatives.
30 *Lai la!:* a shortened form of the Koranic prayer, "La ilaha illa Allah" meaning: "Allah is the sole deity worthy of worship!" In this context it has the emotional ring of exclamation almost bordering on expletive.

Gaan: A Nigerian Pidgin English word, derived from Yoruba, meaning: unmistakably; indisputably; exactly.

31 *Nyash:* Pidgin term for anus, or buttocks generally.
Butu: Pidgin word for squat.
Run four-forty: Pidgin idiom: "to run fast"

32 *Tory:* Pidgin word for story.
Kpokpo-garri: Pidgin: hard, dry, crackly pellets of fried cassava starch.

42 *Na wire o:* Pidgin expression meaning: "It's no joke".
43 *Katakata:* Pidgin word for confusion or confusionist; trouble-maker; a petrel.
Ugbarugba: Pidgin word for calamity.

48 *Patapata:* Pidgin: totally, completely.
49 *Over-sabi:* Pidgin compound word implying overt display of knowledge.

Kola: Short for Kolanut – a pidgin euphemism for bribery.

54 *O ma se o:* Yoruba expression: "What a pity!"
58 *La ku li ju lai lu!:* An exclamation commonly used in Yoruba Moslem circle.
64 *Agedengbe:* Yoruba word for matchet.
66 *Whey:* Pidgin: when; that; who.
Mango-mango: Pidgin: Hanky-panky.
Manafiki: Pidgin: hypocritical; selfishly cunning; treacherous. Derived from the Arabic word Munafiqi.
67 *Una:* Pidgin plural for "you".
Yess: Pidgin for ears.
Wahala: Pidgin for trouble, bother, harassment, inconvenience, discomfort.
68 *Bocoo:* Pidgin: plentiful.

Ogbono soup: a brownish viscous gravy customarily eaten with foo-foo.

Foo-foo: a whitish batter of baked cassava starch.

69 *"Sallallahu alayhi was Sallam"*: Koranic benediction to the Holy Prophet Muhammed: "May blessing and Divine regard be upon him!"

71 *Water don pass garri*: A pidgin expression, "matters are beyond control."

Amin, Ya Rabbi. Barakallah lana wa lakum: Arabic prayer: "Amen, May Allah grant you, too, His blessing."

Alhamdu Lillah: Arabic prayer: "Praise be to Allah!"

72 *Arhamni Ya-Allah*: Arabic prayer: "Shower your blessing on me, O Allah!"

Ami, ami, ami: Yoruba expression: Ámen, amen, amen.

Freedom, Freedom

Prologue and
Act 1 scene III, Act 2 scenes III and VI

Ai remembah when ai was a soljar
Act 1 scene I

"Taxi Driver" Highlife
Act 1 scene III

Oh, people of Nigeria
Act 1 scene V

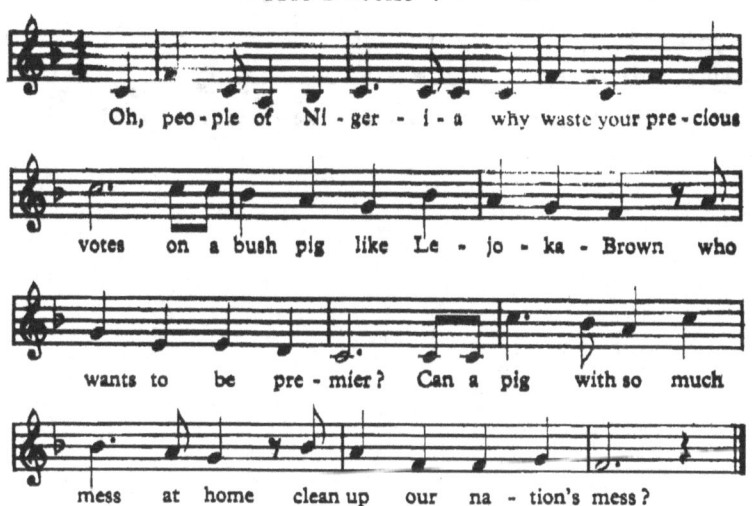

"School Girl" High Life
Act 1 scene V

www.ingramcontent.com/pod-product-compliance
Lightning Source LLC
Chambersburg PA
CBHW011719220426
43663CB00017B/2910